LATE MEDIEVAL
SCOTS POETRY

IACOBVS·I·D·GRATIA·
REX· SCOTORVM

JAMES I OF SCOTLAND

LATE MEDIEVAL SCOTS POETRY

A Selection from the Makars
and their Heirs
down to 1610

Edited with an Introduction,
Notes and Glossary

by

TOM SCOTT

BARNES & NOBLE, INC.
PUBLISHERS · BOOKSELLERS · SINCE 1873

© TOM SCOTT 1967

FIRST PUBLISHED 1967

First published in the United States by Barnes & Noble
New York 10003
Printed in Great Britain by Morrison and Gibb Ltd
London and Edinburgh

CONTENTS

GAWIN DOUGLAS (c. 1475–1522)

SIR DAVID LYNDSAY (? 1490–1555)

RICHARD MAITLAND (1496–1586)

? JAMES V (1513–1590)

ANONYMOUS (? c. 1500)

ALEXANDER SCOTT (? 1520–1590)

INTRODUCTION

I

No man is an island, entire of itself, said John Donne: and neither is any literature, we may add. This is particularly true of the medieval literature of Scotland—or of England. The main unit of society in the Middle Ages was then known as 'Christendom', and it was roughly co-extensive with what is now known as Europe. This 'Christendom' was the spiritual domain of the Roman Catholic Church, to which all member states and countries were subservient. A common belief united them under one authority, even at times under one Emperor, who was to the secular world what the Pope was to the spiritual. As the heirs of the Roman Empire in the West, they had the one literary language, Latin, in common; and with the rise and spread of feudalism, they began to have one social system in common too.

So it was with literature. The parent literary language was Latin: and Latin in the Middle Ages meant such Roman classics as Virgil, Ovid, Lucan, Horace, Statius and others in poetry; Cicero and other classical prose writers; the great philosophic classic of the sixth century, Boethius; and Latin hymns, songs, the Vulgate, sermons, tracts, debates, discourses, and the theological works of such men as John the Scot and, above all, Thomas Aquinas. Out of that literature in Latin grew such developments in the regional languages—mostly dialects of Latin known as 'Romance' languages, but including also such Teutonic ones as German, English, and Scots—as were the foundations of what we now call 'national' literatures. The move from the Middle Ages to the Modern Age, both so-called, is very largely the break-up of the great European state, Christendom, into national states; the accompanying break-up of the Church into national churches; the break-up of the feudal system founded in the wealth of land, and its replacement by the capitalist system founded in the wealth of trade and money; and the emancipation of national literatures in national tongues from the great Latin lingua franca.

Three countries are prominent in the rise of medieval culture, its maturing, and its passing away into what we call the Renaissance, which ushered in the present stage of western civilization. They are France, Italy and Sicily (to call them by their present names, for they were then a complexity of smaller states). Since we are here concerned only with literature, and with poetry in particular, great movements in religion, politics, economics and other dominant strands of life interest us only as they impinge on literature. The most important of these three countries, indeed, the earliest pioneer of each new movement, is the one we now call France, which then included many smaller states, among which Provence was particularly significant from a literary point of view.

The French of the north, with their *langue d'oil* (so named because *oil* or *oui* was its word for 'yes') and the Provençals of the South with their *langue d'oc* (named after its form of 'yes', *oc*) developed a vast poetry during the Middle Ages. All other countries and languages of Europe were and are profoundly indebted to this poetry.

The first great poetic work in the French langauge was the *Chanson de Roland*, a tale of the knights of Charlemagne, but in its wake sprang up many other *gestes* or heroic tales in verse and prose, and romances of Arthur and his knights (centred on what is now Brittany). These were chiefly a northern development—Norman and Breton in character. But in both north and south appeared a cult of love which revolutionized poetry— *amour courtois*. It was already present as part of the chivalric code of the Arthurian romances (the chief poet, Chrétien de Troyes,

2

lived at the court of Marie, Countess of Champagne, who, herself a poet, was a leader of this cult of courtly love). The cult was also the main theme of an astonishing school of lyric poets of Provence, the Troubadours—inventors, that is, of new forms of poetry and song.

Amour courtois was a phenomenon of the life of the castle, which was the centre of feudal life. The castle was left for long periods of time with only the Lady in charge, mistress over a few elderly retainers and young pages, while her Lord was absent on wars, forays, crusades, or other activities of the time. The centre of the cult was a highly artificial and mannered love of the Lady by a young squire or minstrel or the like. It was essentially an adulterous cult, the boy being in love with the wife of his master: it was laid down among the rules of the cult that 'love' could not exist between married partners, since in marriage the woman was the body-slave of the man, his property, whereas in the cult she was an idealized figure, superior in every way to her lover, and her favours could only be won by long supplication, self-abasement, dangerous tasks, and even the health of the lover himself. This dominance of the *dame* is reflected in the rather ambiguous title *midons* by which she was addressed by her *ami*: *midons* in fact means 'my lord' and was the epithet applied to the Lady's husband by his own retainers. The lover had to pine, grow ill, languish to the point of death, faint at sight of the Lady, go mad, rave, etc.—in short behave like a lunatic—in order to prove that his love was genuine and to soften the heart of the Lady into taking pity on his sufferings. On the other hand, if she withheld her favours after being so wooed, or tried to make the excuse of marriage to fend off her lover, she broke the rules of the cult. The 'proper' outcome of the game was that the Lady did in fact eventually sleep with her lover. This game obviously had its dangers, as the husband was apt to be rather jealous of his wifely property. Secrecy therefore was of the essence of the cult, and the worst fault the *ami* could commit was to betray his *dame*.

3

Out of this cult came the most influential poem of the Middle Ages, *Le Roman de la Rose*. It was written by Guillaume de Lorris, who wrote the first 4,070 lines, and Jehan de Meun, who added about four times as many, fifty years later, but in a more satiric vein. The pure poetry of the Rose is in Guillaume alone, and it was written early in the thirteenth century.

This first part of the poem is an allegory of the *amour courtois* cult. The poet falls asleep and dreams that he is in a garden, the garden of the Rose, with whom he is in love (the meaning of the Rose is not simply the Lady, but sexual experience of her) and whose favours he has to win. Various allegorical personages appear, some of them attributes of the Lady, some of them helpers to her favours, some of them dangerous enemies to his love—Pleasure, Sweet-Seeming, Danger, Jealousy, Evil Tongue, Idleness, Reason, Friend, etc. Friend is a very important one here, for the cult allowed for one friend as go-between, a pandar who carried messages to and fro between lover and beloved, and who was sworn to strict secrecy. These are the essential ingredients of the poem: a young lover in love with a great married woman hopelessly out of reach who is guarded by her jealous husband, the lord of the castle of the garden, but not unwilling to be wooed if the young lover is persistent enough and can achieve the tasks she sets him as proof of his love. He has a Friend to help him, and various allegorical personages to help or hinder, repel or ensnare: and his objective is the 'rose', sexual intercourse with the great *dame*. The cult was supposed to bring out the manly and chivalric qualities of the young squire, leading him up and on to fitness for knighthood. This 'love' could not exist between equals, or between unmarried persons, any more than it could between married persons—the Lady must be out of reach, always superior to her grovelling lover. It was clearly a compensatory fantasy born out of the brutalities of feudal marriage in which women were traded like cattle between landed men, partly as symbols of the land that went with them as their dowry, and certainly with no

4

question of 'love' involved at all. Marriage was a property deal between two families or two men of property. What the *ami*—usually a boy in his teens—was in love with, in fact, was the power of his lord, symbolized by his wife. The obvious unbalanced nature of the cult, its parasitic dependence on the brutal feudal marriage for which it was some compensation, the sheer boredom of life in isolated castles, made it a fit instrument of satire in the hands of Jehan de Meun, who took over from Guillaume de Lorris.

This was the great seminal poem of the Middle Ages. The cult of the Lady was paralleled in the religious sphere by the cult of the Virgin, and both were the product of a society and religion in which men were too highly, women too lowly valued. In the *Commedia* of Dante Alighieri, we see the cult of the Virgin blending with that of the *dame* in the figure of Beatrice —and Dante's poem was the first great literary creation in the Italian language, as distinct from Latin. The cult of *amour courtois* itself had a literary root in Latin—in the *Ars Amatoria* of Ovid. The poem of the Rose was read and heard throughout Christendom (among the ruling and educated classes, at least) both in the original and in translations. It would not be too fanciful, though over-simplified, to say that modern English literature began when Geoffrey Chaucer, living a full century after Guillaume and Jehan, and born twenty years after the death of Dante, translated Guillaume de Lorris's part of the Rose into a new literary English which he and others were hammering out of the old Anglo-Saxon as modified by Norman French. Certainly it was in the fourteenth century that English nationalism began to assert itself as such in the reign of the Third Edward, and the national literature took shape in the hands of Chaucer and his contemporaries.

Le Roman de la Rose, however, although it was the chief poem of the ruling-class, was by no means the only kind of poetry: there was also a 'popular' poetry, more realistic, earthy, mundane, enjoyed by a wider public than the courtly one. It was peasant and bourgeois in character, and took the forms of animal fables, ribald stories, comic narratives of lower-class life, religious lyrics even, ballads and songs, religious drama and pageantry. The central poem of this popular genre was the epic fable of *Renart*—Reynard the Fox. This long poem has too many hands in it for any one to be singled out as the 'author', and it seems to have grown somewhere between 1170 and 1250: but it was passed on long after that date like true oral poetry, being added to and subtracted from as it went. The source of this and other fable literature of the Middle Ages was, of course, Aesop.

The origins of the comic narrative poetry are more obscure, but seem to have been a by-product of the Crusades—an Arab influence. This kind of poetry reached its highest peak of achievement not in France, not even in Italy, where Boccaccio, the first professor of Dante studies and an older contemporary of Chaucer, gave the genre a prose form in his *Decameron*, but in England, with *The Canterbury Tales* of Chaucer. Thus, though the French language and national literature was born out of the ruling-class chivalric poetry of *Roland*, Arthurian romance, and the *Rose*; and though the Italian language and national literature was born out of the ruling-class religious epic of Dante; yet English and English national literature, even in what was still an age of chivalry and feudalism, was born out of the mainly middle-class *Canterbury Tales* of Chaucer.

Lyric poetry, short songs to be sung to the lute or other instrument, was common throughout the later Middle Ages. It was both popular and courtly, but was developed chiefly in the schools of Provence and Sicily during the eleventh, twelfth and thirteenth centuries. Almost every lyric form used since in European poetry, and many others long forgotten, were invented and made current during this time by the troubadours. Even the stanza made world-famous by Burns, and known as 'standard Habbie' after its use in the poem lamenting the death of Habbie Simson, is found in the eleventh-century Guillaume, Count of Poitou, the first of the troubadours:

6

Farai un vers de dreyt nien:
Non er di mi ni d'autra gen,
Non er d'amor ni de joven,
        Ni de ren au,
Qu'enans fo trobatz en durmen
        Sobre chevau.

These troubadours influenced Dante, Guido Guinicelli, Guido
Cavalcante and others in Italy, and they were the main source
of the poetry of Petrarch in a later generation. But song was the
matrix of all poetry, and not only the highly wrought art-
songs of the troubadours were current, but Latin lyrics, church
hymns, songs of labour in oral tradition, ballads, dialogues,
debates, satires, pastorals, dawn-songs, serenades, dance-songs,
carols, all abounded and formed the huge corpus of poetry
which is the background to the poems presented in this book.
The Middle Ages have been called an age of faith: this is true,
but they were also a great age of poetry—a fact too little
realized.

II

Out of this wealth of medieval poetry, at the end of the period,
Geoffrey Chaucer was born in the province of European
Christendom which was destined to become the leading nation-
state of the new secular age. Chaucer inherited the poetry of
France and Italy, and began to translate it and re-make much
of it into the new Anglo-Norman language then being hammered
out, of which he became the supreme master. Himself a
bourgeois, son of a vintner in London, but with access to ruling-
class and even royal life as well as his own middle-class, he was
peculiarly fitted both by nature and birth to pillage the literature
of Europe, give it a new and personal impress, and lead the way
forward into the nationalist future.

There are two main ways in which Chaucer influenced later
medieval Scottish poetry. One was simply as one among many

European influences, for Scotland too was a province of European Christendom, more closely linked to France than to England, as a separate kingdom. Guillaume de Lorris, Jehan de Meun, Machaut, Villon, Deschamps, the poets of the Arthurian romances and the Middle-English alliterative romances, Dante, Boccaccio and other Italians, Virgil and the other Latin poets, the troubadours of Provence and court singers of northern France, all influenced the Scottish poets as well as Chaucer, and even through Chaucer as well as directly. Chaucer's contemporary in Scotland, John Barbour, archdeacon of Aberdeen and author of the long poem on Robert Bruce, *The Brus*, was heavily indebted to the French metrical romances. In the next century Henrysoun was indebted to the Reynard poem and Dunbar to many French lyric poets whose forms were sung at court; Douglas translated Virgil, Montgomerie was influenced by the Italians, and James the First was directly influenced by Chaucer, through whom Chaucer's translation of the French *Roman de la Rose* brought in a new wave of French influence.

The second way in which Chaucer influenced the later Scots was much more important than the first, in which Chaucer was but one voice among many, and by no means always the strongest: this second way was by his example as a national poet committed to making a literary language out of the bastard Anglo-Norman spoken round about him. He inspired the Scots to do for their own language what he was doing for English. It was as an English literary nationalist, plundering the continent much as his King Edward the Third was doing materially at the same time, that the example of Chaucer was most fruitful in Scotland. The fact that the Scots langauge—which I shall write about later—is a sister tongue to English made it more accessible to Scotsmen than any continental language, except Latin.

Chaucer's translation of Guillaume's part of the *Rose* (he also translated over three thousand lines of Jehan de Meun's part) is of particular interest to us here. It was one of his earliest works, was widely read in ruling-class circles in his own lifetime, and its influence was even greater in Britain than that of the original. Here are a few lines of the opening of the poem in French, followed by Chaucer's version:

> Ou vintiesme an de mon aage
> Ou point qu'Amors prend le paage
> Des jones gens, couchiez estoie
> Une nuit, si cum je souloie,
> Et me dormoie moult forment,
> Si vi ung songe en mon dormant,
> Qui moult fut biax et moult me plot.
> Mes onques riens ou songe n'ot
> Qui avenu trestout ne soit,
> Si cum li songes recontoit.

> Within my twenty yere of age,
> Whan that love taketh his corage
> Of yonge folk, I wente sone
> To bedde, as I was wont to done,
> And fast I slepe; and in sleping,
> Me mette swiche a swevening,
> That lyked me wonders wel;
> But in that sweven is never a del
> That it nis afterward befalle,
> Right as this dreem wol telle us alle.

Chaucer's version had a deep influence on James the First, who was a prisoner in England from 1405 to 1424, from the age of eleven onwards. His poem, *The Kingis Quair*, is more truly indebted to Chaucer alone than any other Scottish poem; yet how very different it is may be seen at once in the following second stanza, the nearest he gets to echoing the above:

> Quhen as I lay in bed allone waking,
> New partit out of slepe a lyte tofore,
> Fell me to mynd of many diverse thing,
> Off this and that; can I noght say quharfore,

> Bot slepe for craft in erth myght I no more;
> For quhich as tho coude I no better wyle,
> Bot toke a boke to rede apon a quhile.

The reader may care to compare these with other poem-openings, such as those of *The Goldyn Targe* and *The Thrissill and the Rois*, by Dunbar, the first of which is given here (p. 81). King James's poem is in a stanza which Chaucer used elsewhere, rhyme-royal (the name is a translation of the French *chant-royal* and has nothing to do with James's use of it), and not the couplets of the *Romaunt of the Rose* and its original. James, in the last stanza of his 1,379-line poem, acknowledges Gower and Chaucer as his masters and models, thus beginning a fashion among Scots poets which became no more than an insincere convention, often implying that the poet scarcely knew Chaucer, so inept a critical view of him he seems to have, as for example in the last three stanzas of *The Goldyn Targe* (p. 89).

The Kingis Quair is certainly couched in the *Rose* convention, but has many divergences from it. It is not a dream-allegory but a real love-experience with a real woman, Lady Jane Beaufort, who became James's wife and queen of Scots. This shatters the *amour courtois* code, which would not admit the possibility of 'love' in the marriage relationship, but only in adultery. In James's poem—and this is almost the hallmark of Scots poetry—reality takes over from romance. This and other Scots poems of the kind reveal a sharp eye for realistic detail; a moral serious-ness combined with a passionate vigour of utterance outwith the tired convention of the *Rose*; an essentially Christian outlook on marriage, as distinct from the Venus-worship implied by *amour courtois*; and a wealth of fresh nature imagery, often of quite startling brilliance, as in the fourth stanza of *The Goldyn Targe* (p. 82). Chaucer himself, of course, championed married love against the vicious code of *amour courtois* in the *Frankeleynes Tale*, but not in *Romaunt of the Rose*. James, in fact, despite the influence of his English education, was drawing on his deeper inheritance of the realistic tradition of Scots poetry, both popular (*Christis Kirk on the Grene*, the only 'popular' poem given in this book, has been attributed to him) and courtly (as in Barbour's realistic treatment of the romance form as a 'suthfast' story in his *Brus*). A poet's mind is as old as his people and not confined to his ephemeral personality.

The influence of Chaucer, both as national poet and as translator-circulator of the European tradition, is not confined to poetry of the *Rose* type. Much more important for Scottish poetry as well as English was his magnificent paraphrase of Boccaccio's *Il Filostrato*, his *Troilus and Criseyde*. This is a very great poem indeed, as much an original work as a paraphrase, and the one and only begetter of a more original poem than itself, though not a greater—the *Testament of Cresseid* by Robert Henrysoun. Of the three ancient sources of European literature, the Greek, the Roman, and the Hebrew, *Il Filostrato* is drawn from the Greek, the 'matter of Troy', but through Latin versions by the Roman descendants of Troy: for the Caesars claimed descent from Aeneas, prince of Troy, who came to Italy as a refugee. But perhaps the nearest source of Boccaccio's poem is the French *Roman de Troie* by Benôit de Sainte-Maure. It is interesting, in the light of my remarks above on the realism of the Scottish tradition in poetry, to note that Boccaccio altered his sources to achieve greater realism, and passed this on to Chaucer. This is very much a 'Renaissance' trait. But Chaucer's poem, I am persuaded, is a better work than Boccaccio's, and better its instruction. Here is a stanza of *Il Filostrato* (1, 19), followed by what Chaucer made of it:

> Tra li qua' fu di Calcas la figliuola
> Crisëida, quale era in bruna vesta,
> la qual, quanto la rosa la viola
> di biltá vince, cotanto era questa
> piu ch'altra donna, bella; ed essa sola
> piú ch'altra facea lieta la gran festa,
> stando del tempio assai presso alla porta,
> negli atti altiera, piacente ed accorta.

(Among whom was the daughter of Calcas, Criseida, in dark dress who, as much as the rose conquers the violet in beauty, so much was she more beautiful than any other lady; and she alone more than any other made glad the great festival, standing very near the door of the temple, in manner stately, gracious, and agreeable.)

> Among thise othere folk was Criseyda,
> In widewes habite blak; but nathelees
> Right as our firste lettre is now an A,
> In beaute first so stood she, makelees,
> Hir godly looking gladede al the prees.
> Nas never seyn thing to ben preysed derre,
> Nor under cloude blak so bright a sterre. (1, 25)

It cannot be said that Chaucer improves his original here, but the comparative closeness of the paraphrase makes it more useful for our purpose than more creative work.

Henrysoun's poem is no mere imitation of Chaucer's, although it is inspired by it. Indeed, the *Testament of Cresseid* is his own original invention; a story, as far as can be traced, invented by Henrysoun for his own moral purpose of visiting justice on the unfaithful Cresseid. His style is more stark and compact than Chaucer's, but less subtle, except in a few great moments, mostly of psychological drama. His dramatic power exceeds Chaucer's, and is closer, at times, to the Dante of the Inferno. I cannot choose a passage from it which remotely resembles the two passages above, but to support my claims for the poem I choose this stanza in which the blind leper Cresseid is seen by Troilus as he rides past, but only unconsciously recognized:

> Than upon him scho kest up baith her ene,
>   And with ane blenk it come into his thocht
> That he sum tyme hir face befoir had sene;
> Bot scho wes in sic plye he knew hir nocht.
> Yit than hir luik into his mynd it brocht
> The sweit visage and amorous blenking
> Of fair Cresseid, sumtyme his awin darling.

That is great original poetry which could not have been written by anybody but Robert Henrysoun, yet nowhere else in Scottish poetry is the influence of Chaucer more valuably present.

Space forbids further detailed tracing of Chaucer's influence on the later Scots. The *Canterbury Tales* themselves may have influenced such poems as the *Freirs of Berwick*, not included here, and certainly did influence Dunbar's masterpiece, the *Tretis of the tua mariit wemen and the wedo*, which is. It is even alleged that the Wedo herself is drawn from the Wife of Bath. But it has been well said (by Hugh MacDiarmid in his introduction to the Saltire Classics selection of Dunbar's poems) that Dunbar, who has much in common as a poet with Villon, is as unlike Chaucer as one medieval poet could be unlike another. I leave it to the reader to compare and contrast the *Tretis* with the Wife of Bath prologue and tale. Another comparison worth following up is that of Chaucer's and Henrysoun's treatment of Chanteclere and his related characters. The influence of the 'very parfit gentle knyght' *may* have informed also the *Squyer Meldrum* of Sir David Lyndsay, an excerpt from which is given here (p. 141).

III

I have already said that in this book it is possible to present only a few of the very best of the Scots medieval poems. I must now go further and say that (with one exception) we have presented only poems of a certain kind by a certain group of poets. These poets are known collectively by the term *Makars*, which is a Scots translation of the Greek ποιητής, a poet, in its plural form. The term makar, however, was not entirely synonymous with 'poet', but referred to a certain kind of poet—and negatively to a certain other kind or kinds from which it is distinguished. The 'makar' was specifically a poet who regarded a poem as artefact rather than as utterance, message, or vision. The 'makar' was more concerned with the poem as a thing made than as a thing said, and he laboured long and hard over his versification, his metre, his diction and vocabulary, and all the technical side of poetry, aiming at a highly artistic, even artificial, work, rather than simple utterance. I have hinted at this already in quoting Dunbar on Chaucer who, although a superbly conscious craftsman, like most really good poets, subordinated the technical side of his work to what he had to say—his 'sound', to quote Pope, was 'an echo to the sense'. His technique was used to say something, to create patterns of meaningful utterance, not as an object in itself. Now the makars at times tended to regard the patterns of meaningful utterance as something almost incidental to the creation of a beautiful artefact. This is so of Dunbar, though only in certain poems—notably *The Goldyn Targe* and *The Thrissill and the Rois*, only the first of which is given here.

These poets owed a great deal to a French school of poets who had a bigger real influence on them than did Chaucer—the school known as *Les Rhétoriqueurs*. These poets included Guillaume de Machaut (1300–1377), the leading influence; his disciple Eustache Deschamps, a fine lyric poet who wrote down the theories of the new School in his *Art de Dictier* in 1392; Christine de Pisan; Alain Chartier; and Charles d'Orléans (1394–1463), who was a prisoner in England for twenty-five years after his capture at Agincourt, and at whose court the greatest of all French poets of our period, François Villon, briefly stayed. This school took its name from the name they applied to poetic technique—*rhétorique*, and it is significant that their poets were now known as *faiseurs*: our word *makars*, therefore, may owe as much or more to French as or than it does to Greek. These poets concentrated on the poem as artefact. Their forms were intricate and highly artificial (*ballade*, *rondel*, *chant royal*, the *lai*, the *rondeau*, etc.); their language ornate, learned, drawing on Latin classics for new words to naturalize; and their style high-flown. Yet their poetry also tended to be more personal and realistic. Form and content were often at war with each other, and Villon used this tension for some of his effects.

Here surely we find the true antecedents of such a poet as Dunbar. Chaucer imitated Machaut in the *Book of the Duchess*, but it was in shorter forms that Machaut really excelled, and that his influence was most noticeable. It is interesting to note, in passing, that Deschamps, who knew Chaucer, refers to him as *Grant translateur, noble Geoffrey Chaucier*. The influence of this French school was a peculiarly mixed one, making towards highly artificial technique; short and intricate forms; ornate diction; satire; personal realism. The great heir of the movement —it was an early Renaissance one rather than medieval proper, the forms of the old chivalric age clashing with the new bourgeois matter—was François Villon. And Villon's nearest counterpart in any other language is William Dunbar.

The new school of poets in Scotland—new schools would be better, for Dunbar belongs to a very different school from his great predecessor Henrysoun—should be seen against the background of the older schools. The opposite approach to poetry from that of the makars, who saw the poet as a practical artist 'making' a piece of work, is that of the visionaries, to whom the poet is a seer. Now it is interesting that the first of Scottish poets, indeed the archetypal figure of Scottish poets, was one Thomas of Ercildoune (Earlston), known as the Rhymer. Only one poem ascribed to him has come down to us, a high romance on the theme of Tristan and Isolda—*Sir Tristrem*. This is a noble thirteenth-century poem (it was edited by Walter Scott, who first brought it to modern attention) known only to scholars and specialists. But Thomas is the subject of several ballads and legends which make him a figure of folklore, a possession of the entire race. All these ballads and legends agree about one thing: he was a man of supernatural gifts, a seer and a prophet, a poet at the opposite pole from the makars—no practical craftsman merely, but an inspired muse-poet, the very archetype of the muse-poet. This type of poet—the outstanding contemporary example is Robert Graves—is no mere craftsman, though like all good poets he is a superb craftsman as well, but a visionary inspired by a personal intimacy with the Muse herself, the primordial and eternal goddess of poetry. To them, poetry is a form of religious worship of which not God but the Muse is the object. Thomas is so much the type of the muse-inspired poet that the ballads tell how he was spirited away by the goddess herself—the queen of fairyland, they call her—and had to serve her for seven years before he won back to earth. She gave him a gift as reward for his daring to kiss her and enter into her service—a 'tongue that can never lee'.

Other tales of Thomas allege various prophecies of him: he is said to have foretold Flodden and Bannockburn, and much else. This is the typical stuff of folklore, and need not detain us here. What is certain is that there really lived a man in the thirteenth century who was called Thomas Rhymour, or *the* Rhymer, who was born at or lived in Earlston, and who impressed his contemporaries with gifts of supernatural insight, of vision, prophecy, the 'second sicht', so that he became an awesome and legendary figure within a few years of his own death. Whether or not he wrote *Sir Tristrem*, he was a Poet, not a Makar. Any reader who wants to follow up this view of the nature of poetry and poets should read *The White Goddess* by Robert Graves.

Thomas is too shadowy a figure, his poetry too little known, to be compared with the makars in detail, but the same view of poetry informed the work of a very different man, John Barbour, archdeacon of Aberdeen, and an almost exact contemporary of Chaucer. Now Barbour was no visionary poet, no prophet, no seer in the higher sense like Thomas; but he held to the essential trait of such poets—he had 'the tongue that can never lee'. That is of course not to be taken literally, but it does express the highest aim of Barbour, as of other such poets—to tell the truth as they see it. Barbour was a highly educated, highly intelligent man of the world, and truth for him meant not so much supernatural things as the truth of history and ordinary life around him. In his great epic romance of Bruce and the Wars of

Independence, he sought to put down all that he really knew, or had authority to believe, neither adding to it nor taking away. At the very beginning of the *Brus* he tells us that while stories that are purely imaginative can be 'delytabill', those that are 'suthfast' are even more so—and although he is using the romance form, his aim will be the truth and nothing but the truth. This aim of course is incompatible with a highly artificial style—*rhétorique* is its deadliest enemy. Barbour in fact compiled a great history-poem out of old records of the Stewart and other families, making of Bruce's campaigns a military manual which still had validity as a sheer practical guide to the art of war as late as Flodden. If James the Fourth of Scotland had known his Barbour as well as he ought to have done, the worst mistakes of that battle would have been avoided. The English won their great victories against the French—Crecy and Agincourt in particular—because they knew the art of war as Barbour knew it, and the French did not.

The entire works of the makars, on the other hand, would neither have saved nor lost so much as a hair of a war-horse's tail in any battle. There is no reason why they should, of course, but it does help to bring out the difference between the school of Barbour and that begun in Scotland some twenty or thirty years after his death by James the First. Since the scope of this volume, which is confined almost entirely to the Makars, does not permit inclusion of a selection from Barbour, I will give a small sample here of his remarkable quality:

> A! Fredome is a noble thing!
> Fredome makis man to have liking!
> Fredome all solace to man givis:
> He livis at ease that freely livis!
> A noble heart may have nane ease,
> Na ellis nocht that may him please,
> Gif fredome failye; for free liking
> Is yearnit owre all other thing.
> Na he, that ay has livit free,

May nocht knaw weill the propertie,
The anger, na the wrechit doom,
That is couplit to foul thirldom.
Bot gif he had assayit[1] it,
Than all perquer[2] he suld it wit[3];
And suld think fredome mair to prize
Than all the gold in warld that is.

IV

It is impossible to do anything like justice to the vast question
of metric posed by the Makars in the scope of this introduction,
but some comment on the forms used in the poems here presented
is necessary. Of the two main strands of metrical tradition in
Scots poetry, the Teutonic and the Romance, only Dunbar's
Tretis belongs to the former: the rest are all in the Romance,
and that means chiefly French, tradition.

The stanza used by James the First in *The Kingis Quair*, was,
as I have said, derived from the French *chant-royal* in name, not
from its use by James. The form was used by Machaut, Froissart,
Deschamps and Charles d'Orléans, among others, but James
almost certainly derived it from its use by Chaucer in *Troilus
and Criseyde*. Dunbar and Henrysoun also used it in poems of
theirs not included here, and the latter, following Chaucer,
in the *Testament of Cresseid*.

The octosyllabic octave of Henrysoun's *Abbay Walk* derives
from a *ballade* form used by the Troubadours, and common in
French poetry. With a variant of only three stresses in the second,
fourth, sixth, and eighth lines, it is the form used also in *Robene
and Makyne*, and the five-stress longer form of it is that used in
In Prais of Aige. These staple French forms recur throughout
Scottish poetry.

The nine-line stanza of *The Goldyn Targe*, like the Complaint
of Cresseid in the *Testament*, is a rare French form, but it is
found in Gautier d'Espinal as early as the thirteenth century.

[1] experienced   [2] by heart   [3] know

Dunbar's metrical range was immense, and the interested reader is referred to my *Dunbar: a Critical Exposition of the Poems* (Oliver & Boyd, 1966) for a fuller treatment of his metric. *The Tretis of the tua mariit wemen and the wedo* is in a late form of the Anglo-Saxon alliterative measure, taking liberties with the rules of the form which no Anglo-Saxon poet of the heroic period would have allowed himself. For instance, the strict line consisted of two hemistychs of two stresses each, alliterating on the first, perhaps the second, the third, but never on the fourth stress thus: mícle méarc-stàpan móras héaldan. Dunbar alliterates all through the line and often into the next line and even into the third:

> All grathit in to garlandis of fresche gudlie flouris
> So glitterit as the gold wer thair glorius gilt tressis
> Quhill all the gressis did gleme of the glaid hewis.

Note also the piling-up of alliterative effects in fresche . . . flouris, and the double alliterative effects of glitterit, glorius, gleme, glaid. One of the interesting features of Dunbar's metric is that in it one can trace a blending of the two traditions of metre and alliteration in almost every poem:

> For feir of this   all day I drowp
> No gold in kist   nor wyne in cowp
> No ladeis bewtie   nor luiffis blys . . .

See *Meditatioun in Wyntir*.

The couplet form derives from the French early romances, and other forms used by Dunbar and other makars—*rime couée*, rondel, ballade, rondeau, triolet, are all derived from the French lyric poets—probably from French songs commonly sung at court. The five-line stanza of the poem quoted above, a favourite of Dunbar's, is found in Molinet, Gréban, Coquillart and others. The refrain was a common device of French poetry, and Dunbar used it much and variously. The most powerful of his refrains, *Timor mortis conturbat me*, is taken from the Latin

Offices for the Dead, whence Lydgate also derived it for use in a poem of his—much inferior to Dunbar's *Lament*. The reader is invited to compare the refrains of the relevant Dunbar poems presented here, then to follow this through his collected poems.

Of the poems here given by Gawin Douglas there is little of particular metrical note. *The Palice of Honour* nine-line stanza was used by Machault, Chartier and Gringore, and the couplet of his *Aeneid* derives from the romances.

The forms of Lyndsay's *The Dreme* and *Squyer Meldrum* need little comment: the first is in rhyme royal, the same form as *The Kingis Quair*, and the second is in the romance couplet. His great play *Ane Satyre of the Thrie Estaitis* was influenced by Gringore, whose work Lyndsay must have met with during his visit to Paris if not before, but it does not concern us here.

The two poems by Maitland are lyric forms which derive ultimately from the French, but he was much under the influence of Dunbar, particularly in the satire, and of Lyndsay.

The *Chrystis Kirk on the Grene* stanza is one of the most important in Scottish poetry. It dates in Scots from the earlier *Peblis to the Play*, was a favourite stanza of both Fergusson and Burns, who did some of their best work in it, and has been used effectively in our time by Robert Garioch in his *Embro tae the Ploy*, a comic take-off of the Edinburgh Festival. The base of it is simply the octave used by Henrysoun in *Robene and Makyne* with a bob and wheel added—the latter being dropped by Fergusson and Burns. This was a very popular measure in Scots folk poetry, and has been described simply as the 'Scottis meter'.

The Anonymous lyrics presented here are drawn from French models, as are the lyrics of Alexander Scott, who had a feeling for the lighter, more intricate forms, which he handles with a skill unsurpassed in Scots. Scots lyrics are all meant to be sung, and were mostly written to tunes—an art of which Burns is the supreme master, but Alexander Scott is his nearest forebear.

It is well to remember always, in relation to any poetry, that poetry is a sister-art to music—it is meant to be sung or chanted, and is an art of time, not of space. Bearing this always in mind is the surest safeguard against being imposed upon by some of the worst asininities of our time—and of any time—which pretend to see poetry as a spatial art, a principle which, if pursued, would mean the death of poetry. Poetry may be indefinable, but a good working touchstone is this: 'Poetry is verse that sings'.

The stanza used by Montgomerie in his *Cherry and the Slae* is a compilation drawn from French forms. It seems to have been invented in 1556 as a song, *The Banks of Helicon*, and was revived by Burns.

V

A word about the Scots language is also necessary, though only the briefest outline can be given here. The language of the poems presented here is Scots of the Middle Period, a description which implies an early and a 'modern' period. The Scots language as a whole is a development of Old Northumbrian, and in the early period of Scots, from the late thirteenth century (I mean here only written Scots as it has come down to us) to the writing of *The Kingis Quair*, it was almost indistinguishable from the Northumbrian tongue. Of the two main tribes who conquered Britain from Germany, the Saxons occupied mainly the south and west of the country, and the Angles the north. Old Northumbrian developed from this Anglian speech, and was the main speech of an area roughly extending from the Humber to Aberdeen on the East coast, but centred mainly between say Newcastle and Edinburgh. The speech which we now call English developed from an amalgam of Saxon and Norman in the Midlands, chiefly around London and Cambridge, which gradually became the literary dialect of the whole of England. As the borders hardened between Scotland and England, and chiefly as a result of the Wars of Independence from about 1286 to 1314, the Northumbrian speech, comparatively little affected by Norman French, developed into what we now call Scots (Gawin Douglas was the first writer so to name it). Barbour was the great poet of this early period, and his speech is little distinguishable from other Northumbrian poetry of the fourteenth century. The original meaning of the word 'Scots' applied to language was what we now call 'Gaelic', the speech of the Irish Scots who colonized Argyllshire in the sixth century, gradually spreading until the united kingdom of Scotland was established in 884 under the Scots-Pict king Kenneth MacAlpin.

The middle period of Scots, say from 1424, the beginning of the reign of James the First, until roughly 1603, when the Scots king James the Sixth mounted the throne of England in succession to Elizabeth and moved to London to rule his two kingdoms, is the one which concerns us here. Until Douglas transposed the Gaelic title 'Scots' to the speech now so called, meaning the chief dialect of the ruling class of the Scottish nation, not a tribal speech, it was known as 'Ynglis' or 'Inglis'. Dunbar always refers to it by this term, for to him 'Scots' still meant what he called contemptuously 'Erse', (Irish, i.e., Gaelic). But we must not think that Ynglis meant what we mean by English: it meant, strictly, the Anglian tongue, Old Northumbrian, although it is true that Dunbar tended to use it also as a general name for the southern dialect as well. That Scots as used by Henrysoun was a quite distinct tongue from English may best be demonstrated by a small comparison of an English text dating from about 1475, when Henrysoun was about fifty years old, with a passage from his work:

> Myghtfull God veray, Maker of all that is,
> Thre persons withoutten nay, oone God in endles blis,
> Thou maide both nyght and day, beest, fowle, and fysh,
> All creatures that lif may wroght Thou at Thi wish,

As Thou wel myght;
The son, the moyne, verament,
Thou maide, the firmament,
The sternes also full fervent
To shyne Thou maide ful bright.

(Towneley play of Noah)

Ane doolie sessoun to ane cairfull dyte
Suld correspond and be equivalent.
Richt sa it wes quhen I began to wryte
This tragedie, the wedder richt fervent,
Quhen Aries in middis of the Lent;
Schouris of haill can fra the north discend,
That scantlie fra the cauld I micht defend.

(Testament of Cresseid)

The two languages are already as distinct as French and Italian or Spanish, or, more appropriately, Provençal. I have listed elsewhere the main differentiating features of Scots as they affect us here (see p. 189). The close study of the development of Middle English and Early and Middle Scots out of the Anglo-Saxon tongues is a highly specialized and intricate one which at one and the same time establishes the distinct nature of Scots and English from one another, yet sees them in correct perspective as close sister-tongues in one branch of the Teutonic language-tree. It is arguable that Scots is in fact purer English than English is—closer to the original Anglian, less influenced by Norman-French with its high nasality, blurred and weakened consonants, and tendency to reduce all vowels to diphthongs. In Scots the vowels are clear and distinct, sharply differentiated from the diphthongs, and the consonants clean and strong, though in spoken Scots there is the usual popular tendency—specially marked in Cockney—to supplant T with a glo'al stop.

Modern Scots, from Ramsay, Fergusson and Burns up to Hugh MacDiarmid and the present day does not concern us here, but any reader wishing to pursue the study should consult

23

Manual of Modern Scots by Grant and Main Dixon (Cambridge University Press, 1921).

In the poems here presented, the language of James the First in *Kingis Quair* is highly anglicized compared with that of Dunbar or Henrysoun. Henrysoun's language is probably the purest literary norm of the period, and should serve as touchstone for the others. Dunbar had as wide a linguistic range as he had of metric, and three types of diction and style are clearly discernible—usually called his high, middle and low 'styles'. These terms are unsatisfactory and I prefer to call them his courtly manner—the aureate, Latinized and Anglicized manner of *The Goldyn Targe*; his plain manner—that of such meditative poems as *Meditation in Wyntir*; and his popular manner—that of such poems as *In secreit place this hyndir nicht* and some of the dialogue of the *Tretis*, in which he comes close to popular poetry. I will give a line each of these manners to illustrate what I mean: *Up sprang the goldyn candill matutyne* is an example of the courtly manner; *Into thir dirk and drublie dayis* is in the plain manner; and, *I have ane wallidrag, ane worme, ane auld wobat carle* is in the popular manner.

With Gawin Douglas, it may be said, Scots came of age as a national language—and from him it began to decline. Not only did he grasp the fact, and declare it, that the Lothian speech was now a national language with a national literature properly called 'Scots', but his paraphrase of Vergil's *Aeneid* forced him greatly to extend the range and power of Scots diction, borrowing from many other languages to do so. Douglas also brought to perfection a certain trait of Scots poetry, the description of winter, and his winter prologue, given here, is a tour-de-force of the Scots language. There is nothing in English winter poetry that even challenges comparison, although the Scot, James Thomson, comes near it in his poem of Winter, in *The Seasons*.

With David Lyndsay the language is already in a decline, compared with his great predecessors Dunbar and Douglas. This is not merely because he is a lesser poet (he took over

24

Dunbar's satire and carried it to new heights) but because, as a reformer, he was under strong English influence which shows in an anglicization of his language. But his Scots is still a magnificent and distinct instrument. The process of decline can be seen, now faintly, now strongly, in the remaining poets. The language is still fairly pure in Maitland. In *Chrystis Kirk on the Grene* we have the true and superb 'popular' speech, vigorous, simple, strong, and evergreen. The people of Scotland alone kept the language alive in their dialects during the long years of neglect and oppression from the seventeenth century on, so that, when a worthy writer has arisen from the people— Ramsay, Fergusson, Burns, MacDiarmid—he has still had enough of his own native language left to draw on and create true Scottish poetry with, despite the subversive influence of anglicized literati. It is thanks to the people, and mainly the peasantry, that Scots persists to-day, and will persist, as the one pure and indispensable spring of Scottish poetry, always dying and always being re-born. The language of Scott, Montgomerie, Hume and Boyd may not be quite the mighty instrument forged by Dunbar and Douglas, but it is still a pure and unself-conscious Scots, with the breath of eternity in it, the eternal protection of the Muse. As Sorley MacLean, *the* major Gaelic poet since the eighteenth century put it: 'That which once has been forever is'.

VI

With the exception of one poem, all the poetry in this book, and the kind we have been mainly considering, is art-poetry —poetry by, for, or about the ruling and middle classes chiefly. The one exception, although it is said to have been written by a king, is *Chrystis Kirk on the Grene*. This is popular poetry, poetry of and about the folk, influenced by oral tradition. In order to see the Makars against this background, we must take a look at the social milieu of the Scots folk, whose king could write 'folk' poetry.

The Scotland to which James the First returned in 1424 was a small and unstable kingdom, but it was a vigorous and important part of European Christendom. The kingdom had existed for almost six hundred years already, but had been cursed with many afflictions. Among these we may mention the aggressions of Edward the First of England and his son; a succession of infant kings under governing regents, all more or less bad and self-serving; and as a result, the ravages of an uncontrollable pack of ruthless criminals miscalled nobles, who harried the country like wild dogs, enslaved the people, murdered commoners and kings, and even the infant heirs and wives of kings, and laid the kingdom open to its enemies.

James's father came to the throne too old to rule—another curse of the kingdom—as Robert III, and as a result his brother Albany had been allowed a virtual regency. Albany was a typical Scottish baron—ruthless, self-seeking, ambitious, cruel and treacherous. He had imprisoned and starved to death James's elder brother David, the crown prince. It was as a result of this that James had been on his way to France when he was captured by the English, very likely because Albany had informed Henry IV about the ship and its cargo, hoping that the English would slay the young James. Instead, the English imprisoned him for nineteen years and, for a ransom, let him return to Scotland—the most able king of his generation, and the best Stewart ever to hold the sceptre. James's father had died of grief at the news of his capture, and when the young king returned with his English bride to a Scotland in a state of virtual anarchy because of the depredations of the barons, he swore to 'make the key keep the castle and the bush the cow'.

He was as good as his word, executing some of the worst offenders, terrifying others into submission. Scotland knew some semblance of law and justice again, the kingdom began to recover, civilization began to reappear, the barbarian aristocrats were cut down to size—until one of them plotted against the poet-king, trapped him unarmed and alone, and with his fifteen men hacked him to death. Thus died once more the hope of Scotland, after thirteen years of such rule as she had not known since Robert the Bruce died in 1329. It is true that the queen now showed a strength almost equal to her husband's: Graham, the murderous baron, was captured and executed with appalling tortures, spitting in the faces of his executioners as he died. The throne was safe for the time being, but a child was once again on it.

The Kingis Quair was written, it is said, in 1423. Exactly ninety years later James the Fourth died at Flodden. Dunbar the makar died soon after, and Gawin Douglas, his younger contemporary died in 1522 of plague while exiled in London. These ninety-nine years therefore saw the rise, flowering, and decline of the four great makars presented here. What was the country like?

Even by medieval standards Scotland was uncomfortable and uninviting. The shaggy wastes of hill and moor were haunted by wolves, other wild animals, and sometimes wilder men. The garden was the symbol of the human, the cultivated: outside was nature, 'red in tooth and claw'. Trade with the continent was limited to the summer months, late spring and early autumn, because of the dangers of sailing in winter. There were few walled towns, great churches, or large castles. Only Perth and Edinburgh had battlemented walls, the other Royal Burghs having only ports and gatehouses, dykes at the foot of the long narrow roads. Most houses were built of timber and thatch, with middens piled at every door. Cattle were driven through these streets every morning to the common ground outside, and brought back at night, perhaps to share the hovels of their owners. The soil was niggardly, agriculture primitive, crops meagre, and a wet summer meant famine.

The peasants shared their huts with their animals. They were liable to be turned out every five years or so, and thus had no incentive to build houses that would withstand time and weather. Even poverty was insecure. The clergy and gentry were also poor by comparative standards, and the whole country seriously underdeveloped, despite the fact that Scotland had been comparatively peaceful and prosperous during most of the fifteenth century, largely because England was bestowing her imperialist attentions elsewhere. No English army had crossed the border since 1385, until the English raids on Forth and Tay in 1481–1482.

Large houses—even palaces, the scene of the 'court' for which so many of the poems here presented were written—were spartan enough. No castle had more than one chair in the hall, the floors were rush-covered, the rooms dark, ceilings low-raftered, windows small with only the upper half glazed. Paint and tapestries brightened the walls of the principal rooms; costly plate was common; log-fires blazed in open fireplaces; bedrooms would be bare of furniture apart from the bed, which might be canopied, with an arras and feather mattress. The court moved from castle to castle to eat up the produce in kind, moving on when the provisions had been consumed, or when the stench from the ordure that gathered around the castle-walls grew too much for even the most seasoned nose.

Disease was rampant, life short. Leprosy was still common, and so were many other diseases, caused by the omnipresent filth in the towns, which were indeed public middens with houses in them. Towards the end of the fifteenth century plague swept the whole Edinburgh area, schools were closed, children forbidden the streets, merchants to set up booths, and the town barred to incomers under penalty of death. Special cleansers were appointed and paid at danger-money rates—a shilling a day—but the old state of filth soon returned. The poem by Dunbar to the Merchants of Edinburgh is relevant here. The kirkyairds were general dumping-grounds, public lavatories, pastures for sheep and pigs, scenes of dancing and gaming and wenching, and in one case at Aberdeen, even of shipbuilding.

The tolbooth of a town was often the scene of displayed limbs, nailed ears, scourgings and pilloryings, brankings, creelings, tortures, and executions. The rise of capitalism with its eye to the main chance—'singular proffeit', Dunbar calls it—encouraged the custom of large-scale fining (an old idea, of course, but now finding a re-birth) because whereas other forms of punishment were often quite costly to the authorities, this was *pure* gain. For the poorest workers, however, exploited in every possible way by their rulers, the already overburdened flesh had to pay.

These workers produced the wealth for merchants to trade with, barons to steal for their worthless pastimes, and the clergy to spirit away to Rome while parish kirks were scarcely even kept in repair. They went in rags, half-starved, half-naked, begging in the streets. The merchants had almost complete, certainly corrupt control of the burghs, as they were able to manipulate finance for the king and the barons. They made the burgh a closed shop and kept the craftsmen under their mercenary thumbs, and the ordinary people slaves in all but name. Dunbar lashed them unmercifully for their crimes against the people.

Workmen were forced to labour as long as there was light in summer, and even when there was not in winter. A sixteen-hour day was normal, and in 1469 an act was passed against the workers having too many Holy Days, which were said to be bad for the 'national' economy (meaning ruling-class greed). The slaves were to produce more for their masters, not idle about worshipping God in religious festivities. Dunbar, who was at heart a middling-good and very intelligent Christian, sinful, imperfect, but fundamentally sincere, was outraged by the social injustices he saw all round him, and rails against them in satire after satire. He was the first voice of the Reformation in Scottish poetry, and in this he was succeeded by Sir David Lyndsay, whose great play *Ane Satyre of the Thrie Estaitis* was the literary prelude to the Reformation itself.

It has been customary to regard the reign of James the Fourth as a sort of Golden Age in Scotland. It was nothing of the kind. There are no 'golden ages', only gilded ones invented by bad historians. Scotland it is true shared in the far-reaching changes which were fermenting all over Europe, some progressive, some regressive: there was quickening in some directions, and deadening in others. In James she had a typical Stewart ruler—a man of strength and charm, generous of impulse, talented, active, a roaring extrovert given to hunting and seduction. But he was also irresponsible, lacking in statecraft, quixotic, credulous, a bad general who might have been a good cavalry trooper, and the one talent he conspicuously lacked was the difficult one of level-headed kingship. The truth about the age is to be found in the pages of Dunbar, not those of the official historians. The end of the reign in the disastrous folly of Flodden was no accident—it was the almost inevitable outcome of James's character, the bad traits in it ultimately triumphing over the good. The qualities most necessary in kingship in those days were those we might find in a man who is a blend of good general, judge, and higher civil servant.

Dunbar lived at the court of this king as a sort of hanger-on. He was no poet-laureate—Scotland never had one—though the old Celtic tradition of bardship still gave him a certain standing at court. The tradition was too far decayed to help him much, but it does account for the fact that he was allowed to speak very openly to the king—a vestige of the old privilege remained. But an old-time bard did not wheedle—he commanded, and God help anybody who slighted him. Dunbar probably owed as much to the essentially democratic nature of Scottish life as to the bardic tradition. Kings were folk first and kings after. They mixed with the folk, lived among the folk, were closer to the folk than ordinary barons were, went among them in disguise to keep in touch with what was being said and done (and for disguised seduction), and they allowed great freedom of speech to their courtiers. It was this 'popular' nature of the court life that made it possible for Knox to bully

Mary as he did, and for Andrew Melville to tell his august majesty James the Sixth of Scotland and First of England to his face that he was 'but God's silly vassal'. Imagine an English prelate saying any such thing to Henry the Eighth!

Dunbar wrote many poems to the king, some open, some veiled. *His panefull purs* (p. 107) jocularly begs for money from James, who was very mean to Dunbar while promoting utter scoundrels over his head to church benefices. In *Remonstrance to the king* (p. 109) he complains of his ill-treatment at court, gives a remarkably accurate and spirited account of his own worth, and actually threatens the king with a satirical outburst in the manner of an ancient bard if he doesn't attend to Dunbar's needs. In the little poem *On his heid-ake* (p. 117) he apologises for being unable to write something he had promised because of a migraine. And in the *Petition of the gray horse, auld Dunbar* (p. 113) he makes one of the greatest poems ever written out of a plea for a new coat at Christmas. If a new reader of this poem can open his imagination to it fully, and not feel the slightest pinprick in his eyeball, he is either very tough, or the Muse has passed him by.

Dunbar had much better relations at court with the child queen (she was thirteen when she was traded to the thirty-year-old James by her father Henry VII for political reasons) Margaret Tudor. To her he seems to have been a father-figure, grey-haired, tender, kindly, deferential and protective, making her feel at once a queen and yet also a child to be indulged—surely a sympathetic role for an elderly poet. His poems about or to the queen are all characterized by a simple happiness, a relaxed pleasure, except for one terrible one about venereal disease (and I exclude from these remarks *The Tretis of the tua marrit wemen and the Wedo*, which I strongly suspect was written to amuse the queen). One of the best of these is the *Dance in the quenis chalmer* (p 111), which has a delightful picture of Dunbar as a nimble dancer. Is it coincidence that he dances as sure-footedly in his verse? Anyway, the poems of Dunbar tell us more about the court of James the Fourth and the state of Scotland at this time than we can learn from any other source—and, as becomes a poet, more truthfully.

The two poems we give from David Lyndsay's *The Dreme* (pp. 135–37) also speak eloquently of the state of Scotland, but of the later age of James the Fifth.

VII

Behind, under, around, and through the art-poetry of court and cloister which we are mainly concerned with here was the eternal poetry of the folk—the folk whom we have seen 'dreeing their weird' in the appalling conditions sketched out above. The ballads of the border shires (mainly) are of course famous all over the world, and are a part not only of Scottish, not only of British, not only of European, but of world literature. These ballads belong to a very different tradition from literature proper, which means 'written' literature: they are part of the oral tradition, or 'tradition' proper. Ballads only become 'literature' at all when they are written down, and the process of writing them down began, with any seriousness, only in the late seventeenth century. But ballads had been circulating for centuries before that in one form or another, though most of ours are in stanzas developed in Europe in the early stages of our period—and are still circulating. Many of the famous border ballads are mentioned in *The Complaynt of Scotland* (anonymous) written about 1550, and Mr. Hamish Henderson of the School of Scottish Studies in Edinburgh, and other collectors, has and have recorded versions of them still being sung among the folk.

These ballads and other oral poetry sung and recited and passed on by ear are not to be thought of as something strictly apart from art-poetry: the two kinds interpenetrate each other. The audience for the art-poetry would be just as well-versed in and appreciative of the folk-poetry, and some at least of the forms and themes of art-poetry went down to the people, who could not read. Some of the refrains of Dunbar read very like ballad refrains. The *Lament quhen he was seik* given here has the stark elemental quality of some of the best ballads: conversely, some of the great ballad stanzas might have been the work of Dunbar, so great is their classical art. The world of Henrysoun's fables is essentially a folk world: and what is that great poem *The Testament of Cresseid* if not a great ballad in highly literary form?

But ballad was not the only kind of folk poetry current in our period. There were songs of all sorts, carols, work-songs, dances with words to them, tales, joke-poems, fables, love-songs, laments, and so on. One of these, *Kynd Kyttok*, has long been attributed without rhyme or reason to Dunbar. It tells of the author's grandmother who liked a good drink in her day, and when she went to heaven after death found the ale of heaven too sour, so she stole out for a decent drink 'back home': Saint Peter 'hat her with a club' when she returned, and God 'leuch his hert sair' to see her let in. There were also anonymous tales which were full of the folk spirit—*Golagros and Gawain, Rauf Colyeir, Cokelbeis Sow*—and seem to have been a meeting-place for the oral and literary traditions, being at once 'popular' and highly literate. In them the racy, earthy Scots runs vigorous and pure, in contradistinction to the decadent 'aureate' tradition of such poem-tapestries as *The Goldyn Targe*.

Among these 'popular' poems are two anonymous poems which tradition persists in attributing to James the Fifth (some have said James the First). These poems are *Peblis to the Play*, and *Chrystis kirk on the Grene*. They are in the same stanza form and of much the same spirit, but I think *Chrystis kirk* is the better of the two. This poem has been included here (p. 150) as a reminder of the 'folk', and to make the point that Scottish kings had no lack of the 'common touch'.

BIBLIOGRAPHICAL NOTES

THE texts used in this book are indicated at the end of each poem, and they are listed here more fully, with one or two others which may be useful.

The Kingis Quair. Edited by Mackay Mackenzie, Faber & Faber, 1939.

The Poems and Fables of Robert Henrysoun. Edited by H. Harvey Wood, Edinburgh, 1933.

The Poems of William Dunbar. Edited by Mackay Mackenzie, Faber & Faber, 1932.

Selected Poems of Gawin Douglas. Edited by Sydney Goodsir Smith, Saltire Classics, Oliver & Boyd, Edinburgh.

Selections from Gawin Douglas. Edited by David F. C. Coldwell, The Clarendon Press, Oxford.

The Works of Sir David Lyndsay. Edited by D. Hamer for Scottish Texts Society, Blackwood, 1931–1936.

A selection of the poems edited by Maurice Lindsay for the Saltire Classics series can be had from the Saltire Society, Gladstones Land, Edinburgh, or through bookshops. There is also a text of *Ane Satyre of the Thrie Estaitis*, edited by J. Kinsley, 1954, and of *Squyer Meldrum* by the same editor.

All other poems are from the Scottish Texts Society publications, unfortunately not easily obtainable except through libraries. Of these, the poem by Walter Kennedy is from Volume II of the STS edition of the Bannatyne Manuscript; the first two Anonymous lyrics are from the same edition. *Chrystis Kirk on the Grene* is from the STS edition of the Maitland Folio, and the third Anonymous lyric is from the STS edition of the Maitland Quarto. All the poems by Alexander Scott, Montgomerie, and Alexander Hume are from the STS editions of their collected works. Selections from the first two are also to be had from the Saltire Society, address above. The Boyd Sonet is from the MS in National Library of Scotland.

For much of the background material in the Introduction I wish to acknowledge a debt of gratitude to the authors of the following works:

HISTORICAL BACKGROUND

Wm. Croft Dickinson, *Scotland from the Earliest Times to* 1603, Edinburgh, 1961.

R. L. Mackie, *King James the Fourth of Scotland*, Edinburgh, 1958.

W. Mackay Mackenzie, *The Secret of Flodden*, Edinburgh, 1961.

R. H. Tawney, *Religion and the Rise of Capitalism*, Murray, 1926.

These are the main historical works drawn on here, but many others exert a general influence, notably various historical works by Agnes Mure Mackenzie, R. L. Mackie, G. M. Thomson, and Hume Brown.

LITERARY AND CRITICAL BACKGROUND

C. S. Lewis, *The Allegory of Love*, Oxford, 1936.

Bruce Pattison, *Music and Poetry of the English Renaissance*, London, 1948.

John Stevens, *Music and Poetry in the Early Tudor Court*, London, 1961.

W. G. Dodd, *Courtly Love in Chaucer and Gower*, Harvard, 1913.

W. A. Neilson, *The Origins and Sources of the Court of Love*, Harvard Studies, VI, 1899.

J. Schipper, *Old English Metric*, 2 vols., Bonn, 1882–1888.

Thomas S. Omond, *A Study of Metre*, 1903.

George Saintsbury, *A History of English Prosody*, 1906.

P. F. Baum, *Principles of English Versification*, Harvard, 1922.

John Thompson, *The Founding of English Metre*, London, 1961. This study of English metric from 1557 to the late Elizabethan period is highly recommended.

James Colville, *Studies in Lowland Scots*, Edinburgh, 1909.

J. A. H. Murray, *Dialects of the Southern Counties of Scotland*, Edinburgh, 1873.

G. Gregory Smith, *Specimens of Middle Scots*, Edinburgh, 1902.

David Irving, *Lives of the Scottish Poets*, Edinburgh, 1803.

Society of Ancient Scots, *Lives of the Scottish Poets*, London, 1822. Difficult to get, but highly recommended.

Janet M. Smith, *The French Background of Middle Scots Literature*, Edinburgh, 1934. Highly recommended.

35

Kurt Wittig, *The Scottish Tradition in Literature*, Edinburgh, 1958. The best study to date, but incomplete.

James Kinsley, *Scottish Poetry: A Critical Survey*, London, 1955. Highly recommended.

C. S. Lewis, *English Literature in the Sixteenth Century*, in the *Oxford History of English Literature*, Oxford, 1954.

John Spiers, *The Scots Literary Tradition*, London, 1940 and 1961.

J. H. Millar, *A Literary History of Scotland*, London, 1903.

G. Gregory Smith, *Scottish Literature*, London, 1919.

G. Gregory Smith, *The Transition Period*, Edinburgh, 1900. An important study of fifteenth century European literature.

Charles Muscatine, *Chaucer and the French Tradition*, University of California Press, 1957. Highly recommended.

Other works of Scottish, English and European literary background are too numerous to mention and their influence too general for specific notice. The editor is indebted to Professor John MacQueen for some of the textual readings here presented, notably those from the Bannatyne MS, and Maitland MSS.

JAMES I

From *The Kingis Quair*

Cantus

'Worschippe, ye that loveris bene, this May,
   For of your bliss the kalendis ar begonne,
And sing with us, away, winter, away!
   Cum, somer, cum, the suete sesoun and sonne!
   Awake for schame that have your hevynnis wonne,
And amorously lift up your hedis all,
Thank lufe that list you to his merci call.'

Quhen thai this song had song a lytill thrawe,
   Thai stent a quhile, and therewith unaffraid,
As I beheld and kest myn eyne alawe,   10
   From beugh to beugh thay hippit and thai plaid,
   And freschly in thair birdis kynd arraid
Thair fetheris new, and fret thame in the sonne,
And thankit lufe, that had thair makis wonne.

This was the plane ditee of thair note,
   And therewithall unto myself I thoght,
'Quhat lyf is this, that makis birdis dote?
   Quhat may this be, how cummyth it of ought?
   Quhat nedith it to be so dere ybought?
It is nothing, trowe I, bot feynit chere,   20
And that men list to counterfeten chere.'

37

Eft wald I think; 'O Lord, quhat may this be?
   That lufe is of so noble myght and kynde,
Lufing his folk, and suich prosperitee
   Is it of him, as we in bukis fynd?
   May he oure hertes setten and unbynd?
Hath he upon oure hertis suich maistrye?
Or all this is bot feynyt fantasye!

For gif he be of so grete excellence,
   That he of every wight hath cure and charge,   30
Quhat have I gilt to him or doon offens,
   That I am thrall, and birdis gone at large,
   Sen him to serve he myght set my corage?
And gif he be noght so, than may I seyne,
Quhat makis folk to jangill of him in veyne?

Can I noght elles fynd, bot gif that he
   Be Lord, and as a God may lyve and regne,
To bynd and lous, and maken thrallis free,
   Than wold I pray his blisfull grace benigne,
   To hable me unto his service digne;   40
And evermore for to be one of tho
Him trewly for to serve in wele and wo.'

And therwith kest I doun myn eye ageyne,
   Quhare as I sawe, walking under the tour,
Full secretly new cummyn hir to pleyne,
   The fairest or the freschest yong floure
   That ever I sawe, me thoght, before that houre,
For quhich sodayn abate, anon astert,
The blude of all my body to my hert.

And though I stude abaisit tho a lyte   50
   No wonder was, forquhy my wittis all

Were so ouercom woth plesance and delyte,
    Onely throu latting of myn eyen fall,
    That sudaynly my hert become hir thrall
For ever of free wyll; for of manace
There was no takyn in hir suete face.

And in my hede I drewe ryght hastily,
    And eftsones I lent it forth ageyne,
And sawe hir walk, that verray womanly,
    With no wight mo bot onely women tueyne.   60
    Than gan I studye in myself and seyne,
'A! suete, ar ye a warldly creature,
Or hevinly thing in likeness of nature?

Or ar ye god Cupidis owin princesse,
    And cummyn ar to lous me out of band?
Or ar ye verray nature the goddess,
    That have depaynted with your hevinly hand
    This gardyn, full of flouris, as they stand?
Quhat sall I think, allace! quhat reverence
Sall I minster to your excellence?   70

Gif ye a goddess be, and that ye like
    To do me payne, I may it noght astert;
Gif ye be warldly wight, that dooth me sike,
    Quhy lest God mak you so, my derrest hert,
    To do a sely prisoner thus smert,
That lufis yow all, and wote of noght bot wo?
And therfore, merci, suete! sen it is so.'

(Mackenzie, *The Kingis Quair*)

39

Quhare, in a lusty plane, tuke I my way,
  Endlang a ryver, plesant to behold,
Enbroudin all with fresche flouris gay,
  Quhare, throu the gravel, bryght as ony gold,
  The cristall water ran so clere and cold,
That in myn ere maid contynualy
A maner soun, mellit with armony;

That full of lytill fischis by the brym,
  Now here, now there, with bakkis blewe as lede,
Lap and playit, and in a rout can swym   10
  So prattily, and dressit tham to sprede
  Thair curall fynnis, as the ruby rede,
That in the sonne on thair scalis bryght
As gesserant ay glitterit in my sight:

And by this ilke ryversyde alawe
  Ane hye way fand I like to bene,
On quhich, on every syde, a long rawe
  Off treis saw I, full of levis grene,
  That full of fruyte delitable were to sene,
And also, as it come unto my mind,   20
Off bestis sawe I mony divers kynd:

The lyoun king, and his fere lyonesse;
  The pantere, like unto the smaragdyne;
The lytill squerell, full of besyness;
  The slawe as, the druggar beste of pyne;
  The nyce ape; the werely porpapyne;
The percyng lynx; the lufare unicorne,
That voidis venym with his evour horne.

There sawe I dress him new out of haunt
  The fery tiger, full of felonye;   30
The dromydare; the standar oliphant;
  The wyly fox the wedowis inemye;
  The clymbare gayte; the elk for alblastrye;
The herknere bore; the holsum grey for hortis;
The hair also, that oft gooth to the wortis.

The bugill, drawar by his hornis grete;
  The martrik, sable, the foynyee, and mony mo;
The chalk-quhite ermyn, tippit as the jete;
  The riall hert, the conyng, and the ro;
  The wolf, that of the murthir noght say 'ho!'   40
The lesty bever, and the ravin bare;
For chamelot the camel full of hare;

With mony an othir beste divers and strange,
  That cummyth noght as now unto my mynd.
Bot now to purpos—straucht furth the range
  I held a way, ourhailing in my mynd
  From quhens I come, and quhare that I suld fynd
Fortune, the goddess, unto quhom in hye
Gude Hope, my gyde, has led me sodeynly.

And at the last, behalding thus asyde,   50
  A round place wallit have I found;
In myddis quhare eftsone I have spide
  Fortune, the goddess, hufing on the ground;
  And ryght before hir fete, of compas round,
A quhele, on quhich clevering I sye
A multitude of folk before myn eye.

And ane surcote sche werit long that tyde,
  That semyt to me of divers hewis,
Quhilum thus, quhen sche wald turn asyde,

Stude this goddess of fortune and [of glewis];   60
    A chapellet with mony fresche anewis
Sche had upon her hed; and with this hong
A mantill on hir schuldris, large and long,

That furrit was with ermyn full quhite,
    Degoutit with the self in spottis blake:
And quhilum in hir chier thus a lyte
    Louring sche was; and thus sone it would slake,
    And sodeynly a maner smylyng make,
And sche were glad; at one contenance
Sche held noght, bot ay in variance.   70

And underneth the quhele sawe I there
    Ane ugly pit depe as ony helle,
That to behald thereon I quoke for fere;
    Bot o thing herd I, that quho therein fell
    Com no more up agene tidingis to telle;
Off quhich, astonait of that ferefull syght,
I ne wist quhat to done, so was I fricht.

Bot for to se the sudayn weltering
    Off that ilk quhele, that sloppar was to hold,
It semyt unto my wit a strong thing,   80
    So mony I sawe that than clymben wold,
    And failit foting, and to ground were rold;
And othir eke, that sat abone on hye,
Were ouerthrawe in twinklyng of an eye.

And on the quhele was lytill void space,
    Wele nere ourstraught fro lawe to hye;
And they were war that long sat in place,
    So tolter quhilum did sche it to-wrye;
    There was bot clymbe and ryght dounward hye,
And sum were eke that fallyng had sore,   90
Therefor to clymbe thair corage was no more.

42

I sawe also that, quhere sum were slungin,
  Be quhirlyng of the quhele, into the ground,
Full sudaynly sche hath up ythrungin,
  And set thame on agene full sauf and sound:
  And ever I sawe a new swarm abound,
That to clymbe upward upon the quhele,
In stede of thame that myght no langer rele.

(Mackenzie edition)

ROBERT HENRYSOUN

The Testament of Cresseid

Ane doolie sessoun to ane cairfull dyte
Suld correspond, and be equivalent.
Richt sa it wes quhen I began to wryte
This tragedie, the wedder richt fervent,
Quhen Aries, in middis of the Lent,
Schouris of haill can fra the north discend,
That scantlie fra the cauld I micht defend.

Yit nevertheles within myne oratur
I stude, quhen Titan had his bemis bricht
Withdrawin doun, and sylit under cure   10
And fair Venus, the bewtie of the nicht,
Uprais, and set unto the west full richt
Hir goldin face in oppositioun
Of God Phebus direct discending doun.

Throw out the glas hir bemis brast sa fair
That I micht se on everie syde me by
The Northin wind had purifyit the Air
And sched the mistie cloudis fra the sky,
The froist freisit, the blastis bitterly
Fra Pole Artick come quhisling loud and schill,   20
And causit me remufe aganis my will.

For I traistit that Venus, luifis Quene,
To quhome sum tyme I hecht obedience,
My faidit hart of lufe scho wald mak grene,

And therupon with humbill reverence,
I thocht to pray hir hie Magnificence;
Bot for greit cald as than I lattit was,
And in my Chalmer to the fyre can pas.

Thocht lufe be hait, yit in ane man of age
It kendillis nocht sa sone as in youtheid,   30
Of quhome the blude is flowing in ane rage,
And in the auld the curage doif and deid,
Of quhilk the fyre outward is best remeid;
To help be Phisike quhair that nature faillit
I am expert, for baith I have assailit.

I mend the fyre and beikit me about,
Than tuik ane drink my spreitis to comfort,
And armit me weill fra the cauld thairout:
To cut the winter nicht and mak it schort,
I tuik ane Quair, and left all uther sport,   40
Writtin be worthie Chaucer glorious,
Of fair Creisseid, and worthie Troylus.

And thair I fand, efter that Diomeid
Ressavit had that Lady bricht of hew,
How Troilus neir out of wit abraid,
And weipit soir with visage paill of hew;
For Quhilk wanhope his teiris can renew
Quhill Esperus rejoisit him agane,
Thus quhyle in Joy he levit, quhyle in pane.

Of hir behest he had greit comforting,   50
Traisting to Troy that scho suld mak retour,
Quhilk he desyrit maist of eirdly thing
Forquhy scho was his only Paramour;
Bot quhen he saw passit baith day and hour
Of hir ganecome, than sorrow can oppres
His wofull hart in cair and hevines.

Of his distres me neidis nocht reheirs,
For worthie Chauceir in the samin buik
In gudelie termis and in Joly veirs
Compylit hes his cairis, quha will luik.   60
To brek my sleip ane uther quair I tuik,
In quhilk I fand the fatall destenie
Of fair Cresseid, that endit wretchitlie.

Quha wait gif all that Chauceir wrait was trew?
Nor I wait nocht gif this narratioun
Be authoreist, or fenyeit of the new
Be sum Poeit, throw his Inventioun,
Maid to report the Lamentatioun
And wofull end of this lustie Creisseid,
And quhat distres scho thoillit, and quhat deid.   70

Quhen Diomeid had all his appetyte,
And mair, fulfillit of this fair Ladie,
Upon ane uther he set his haill delyte
And send to hir ane Lybell of repudie,
And hir excludit fra his companie.
Than desolait scho walkit up and doun,
And sum men sayis into the Court commoun.

O fair Creisseid, the flour and A per se
Of Troy and Grece, how was thou fortunait!
To change in filth all thy Feminitie,   80
And be with fleschlie lust sa maculait,
And go amang the Greikis air and lait
Sa giglotlike, takand thy foull plesance!
I have pietie thou suld fall sic mischance.

Yit nevertheless quhat ever men deme or say
In scornefull langage of thy brukkilnes,
I sall excuse, als far furth as I may,

46

Thy womanheid, thy wisdome and fairness:
The quhilk Fortoun hes put to sic distres
As hir pleisit, and nathing throw the gilt   90
Of the, throw wickit langage to be spilt.

This fair Lady, in this wyse destitute
Of all comfort and consolatioun,
Richt privelie, but fellowschip, on fute
Disagysit passit far out of the toun
Ane myle or twa, unto ane Mansioun
Beildit full gay, quhair hir father Calchas
Quhilk than amang the Greikis dwelland was.

Quhen he hir saw, the caus he can Inquyre
Of hir cumming; scho said, siching full soir: 100
'Fra Diomeid had gottin his desyre
He wox werie, and wald of me no moir.'
Quod Calchas, 'douchter, weip thou not thairfoir;
Peraventure all cummis for the best;
Welcum to me, thou art full deir ane Gest.'

This auld Calchas, efter the Law was tho,
Wes keiper of the Tempill as ane Preist,
In quhilk Venus and hir Sone Cupido
War honourit, and his Chalmer was thame neist,
To quhilk Cresseid with baill aneuch in breist   110
Usit to pas, hir prayeris for to say.
Quhill at the last, upon ane Solempne day,

As custome was, the pepill far and neir
Befoir the none, unto the Tempill went,
With Sacrifice, devoit in thair maneir:
Bot still Cresseid, hevie in hir Intent,
Into the Kirk wald not hir self present,
For giving of the pepill ony deming
Of hir expuls fra Diomeid the King:

Bot past into ane secreit Orature   120
Quhair scho micht weip hir wofull desteny,
Behind hir bak scho cloisit fast the dure
And on hir kneis bair fell doun in hy.
Upon Venus and Cupide angerly
Scho cryit out, and said on this same wyse,
'Allace that ever I maid you Sacrifice.

'Ye gave me anis ane devine responsaill
That I suld be the flour of luif in Troy,
Now am I maid ane unworthie outwaill,
And all in cair translatit is my Joy,   130
Quha sall me gyde? quha sall me now convoy
Sen I fra Diomeid and Nobill Troylus
Am clene excludit, as abject odious?

'O fals Cupide, is nane to wyte bot thow,
And thy Mother, of lufe the blind Goddes!
Ye causit me alwayis understand and trow
The seid of lufe was sawin in my face,
And ay grew grene throw your supplie and grace.
Bot now allace that seid with froist is slane,
And I fra luifferis left and all forlane.'   140

Quhen this was said, doun in ane extasie,
Ravischit in spreit, intill ane dreame scho fell,
And be apperance hard, quhair scho did ly,
Cupide the King ringand ane silver bell,
Quhilk men micht heir fra hevin unto hell;
At quhais sound befoir Cupide appeiris
The seven Planetis discending fra thair Spheiris,

Quhilk hes power of all thing generabill
To reull and steir be thair greit Influence,
Wedder and wind, and coursis variabill: 150

48

And first of all Saturne gave his sentence,
Quhilk gave to Cupide litill reverence,
Bot, as ane busteous Churle on his maneir,
Come crabitlie with auster luik and cheir.

His face [fronsit], his lyre was lyke the Leid,
His teith chatterit, and cheverit with the Chin,
His Ene drowpit, how sonkin in his heid,
Out of his Nois the Meldrop fast can rin,
With lippis bla and cheikis leine and thin;
The Iceschoklis that fra his hair doun hang   160
Was wonder greit, and as ane speir als lang.

Atouir his belt his lyart lokkis lay
Felterit unfair, ouirfret with Froistis hoir,
His garmound and his gyis full gay of gray,
His widderit weid fra him the wind out woir;
Ane busteous bow within his hand he boir,
Under his girdill ane flasche of felloun flanis,
Fedderit with Ice, and heidit with hailstanis.

Than Juppiter, richt fair and amiabill,
God of the Starnis in the Firmament,   170
And Nureis to all thing generabill,
Fra his Father Saturne far different,
With burelie face, and browis bricht and brent,
Upon his heid ane Garland, wonder gay,
Of flouris fair, as it had bene in May.

His voice was cleir, as Cristall were his Ene,
As goldin wyre sa glitterand was his hair;
His garmound and his gyis full [gay] of grene,
With golden listis gilt on everie gair;
Ane burelie brand about his midill bair;   180
In his richt hand he had ane groundin speir,
Of his Father the wraith fra us to weir.

49

Nixt efter him come Mars, the God of Ire,
Of strife, debait, and all dissensioun,
To chide and fecht, als feirs as ony fyre;
In hard Harnes, hewmound and Habirgeoun,
And on his hanche ane roustie fell Fachioun;
And in his hand he had ane roustie sword;
Wrything his face with mony angrie word,

Schaikand his sword, befoir Cupide he come   190
With reid visage, and grislie glowrand Ene;
And at his mouth ane bullar stude of fome
Lyke to ane Bair quhetting his Tuskis kene,
Richt Tui[l]lyeour lyke, but temperance in tene;
Ane horne he blew, with mony bosteous brag,
Quhilk all this warld with weir hes maid to wag.

Than fair Phebus, Lanterne & Lamp of licht
Of man and beist, baith frute and flourisching,
Tender Nureis, and banischer of nicht,
And of the warld causing, be his moving   200
And Influence, lyfe in all eirdlie thing,
Without comfort of quhome, of force to nocht
Must all ga die that in this warld is wrocht.

As King Royall he raid upon his Chair
The quhilk Phaeton gydit sum tyme upricht;
The brichtnes of his face quhen it was bair
Nane micht behald for peirsing of his sicht.
This goldin Cart with fyrie bemis bricht
Four yokkit steidis full different of hew,
But bait or tyring, throw the Spheiris drew.   210

The first was soyr, with Mane als reid as Rois,
Callit Eoye into the Orient;
The secund steid to Name hecht Ethios,

Quhitlie and paill, and sum deill ascendent;
The third Peros, richt hait and richt fervent;
The feird was blak, callit Philologie
Quhilk rollis Phebus doun into the sey.

Venus was thair present that goddes [gay],
Hir Sonnis querrell for to defend and mak
Hir awin complaint, cled in ane nyce array,   220
The ane half grene, the uther half Sabill black;
Quhyte hair as gold kemmit and sched abak;
Bot in hir face semit greit variance,
Quhyles perfyte treuth, and quhyles Inconstance

Under smyling scho was dissimulait,
Provocative, with blenkis Amorous,
And suddenly changit and alterait,
Angrie as ony Serpent vennemous
Richt pungitive, with wordis odious.
Thus variant scho was, quha list tak keip,   230
With ane Eye lauch, and with the uther weip.

In taikning that all fleschelie Paramour
Quhilk Venus hes in reull and governance,
Is sum tyme sweit, sum tyme bitter and sour
Richt unstabill, and full of variance,
Mingit with cairful Joy and fals plesance,
Now hait, now cauld, now blyith, now full of wo,
Now grene as leif, now widderit and ago.

With buik in hand than come Mercurius,
Richt Eloquent, and full of Rethorie,   240
With polite termis and delicious,
With pen and Ink to report al reddie,
Setting sangis and singand merilie:
His Hude was reid, heklit atouir his Croun,
Lyke to ane Poeit of the auld fassoun.

Boxis he bair with fine Electuairis,
And sugerit Syropis for digestioun,
Spycis belangand to the Pothecairis,
With mony hailsum sweit Confectioun,
Doctour in Phisick cled in ane Skarlot goun, 250
And furrit weill, as sic ane aucht to be,
Honest and gude, and not ane word culd le.

Nixt efter him come Lady Cynthia,
The last of all, and swiftest in hir Spheir,
Of colour blak, buskit with hornis twa,
And in the nicht scho listis best appeir.
Haw as the Leid, of colour nathing cleir;
For all hir licht scho borrowis at hir brother
Titan, for of hir self scho hes nane uther.

Hir gyse was gray, and ful of spottis blak, 260
And on hir breist ane Churle paintit full evin,
Beirand ane bunche of Thornis on his bak,
Quhilk for his thift micht clim na nar the hevin.
Thus quhen thay gadderit war, thir Goddes sevin.
Mercurius thay cheisit with ane assent
To be foirspeikar in the Parliament.

Quha had bene thair, and liken for to heir
His facound toung, and termis exquisite,
Of Rethorick the prettick he micht leir,
In breif Sermone ane pregnant sentence wryte: 270
Befoir Cupide veiling his Cap alyte,
Speiris the caus of that vocatioun,
And he anone schew his Intentioun.

'Lo!' (quod Cupide), 'quha will blaspheme the name
Of his awin God, outher in word or deid,
To all Goddis he dois baith lak and schame,

52

And suld have bitter panis to his meid.
I say this by yone wretchit Cresseid,
The quilk throw me was sum tyme flour of lufe,
Me and my Mother starklie can reprufe.   280

'Saying of hir greit Infelicitie
I was the caus, and my Mother Venus,
Ane blind Goddes, hir cald, that micht not se,
With sclander and defame Injurious;
Thus hir leving unclene and Lecherous
Scho wald returne on me and my Mother,
To quhome I schew my grace abone all uther.

'And sen ye ar all sevin deificait,
Participant of devyne sapience,
This greit Injurie done to our hie estait   290
Me think with pane we suld mak recompence;
Was never to Goddes done sic violence.
Asweill for yow, as for myself I say,
Thairfoir ga help to revenge I yow pray.'

Mercurius to Cupide gave answeir
And said: 'Schir King my counsall is that ye
Refer yow to the hiest planeit heir,
And tak to him the lawest of degre,
The pane of Cresseid for to modifie;
As god Saturne, with him tak Cynthia.'   300
'I am content' (quod he), 'to tak thay twa.'

Than thus proceidit Saturne and the Mone,
Quhen thay the mater rypelie had degest,
For the dispyte to Cupide scho had done,
And to Venus oppin and manifest,
In all hir lyfe with pane to be opprest,
And torment sair, with seiknes Incurabill,
And to all lovers be abhominabill.

This duleful sentence Saturne tuik on hand,
And passit doun quhair cairfull Cresseid lay,   310
And on hir heid he laid ane frostie wand;
Than lawfullie on this wyse can he say:
'Thy greit fairnes and all thy bewtie gay,
Thy wantoun blude, and eik thy goldin Hair,
Heir I exclude fra the for evermair.

'I change thy mirth into Melancholy,
Quhilk is the Mother of all pensiveness;
Thy Moisture and thy heit in cald and dry;
Thyne Insolence, thy play and wantones
To greit diseis; thy Pomp and thy riches   320
In mortall neid; and greit penuritie
Thou suffer sall, and as ane beggar die.'

O cruell Saturne! fraward and angrie,
Hard is thy dome, and to malitious;
On fair Cresseid quhy hes thou na mercie,
Quhilk was sa sweit, gentill and amorous?
Withdraw thy sentence and be gracious
As thou was never; so schawis thow thy deid,
Ane wraikfull sentence gevin on fair Cresseid.

Than Cynthia, quhen Saturne past away,   330
Out of hir sait discendit doun belyve,
And red ane bill on Cresseid quhair scho lay,
Contening this sentence diffinityve;
'Fra heit of bodie I the now depryve,
And to thy seiknes sal be na recure,
Bot in dolour thy dayis to Indure.

'Thy Cristall Ene minglit with blude I mak,
Thy voice sa cleir, unplesand hoir and hace,
Thy lustie lyre ouirspred with spottis blak,

54

And lumpis haw appeirand in thy face.   340
Quhair thou cumis, Ilk man sal fle the place.
This sall thou go begging fra hous to hous
With Cop and Clapper lyke ane Lazarous.'

This doolie dreame, this uglye visioun
Brocht to ane end, Cresseid fra it awoik,
And all that Court and convocatioun
Vanischit away, than rais scho up and tuik
Ane poleist glas, and hir schaddow culd luik:
And quhen scho saw hir face sa deformait
Gif scho in hart was wa aneuch God wait.   350

Weiping full sair, 'Lo quhat it is' (quod sche),
'With fraward langage for to mufe and steir
Our craibit Goddis, and sa is sene on me!
My blaspheming now have I bocht full deir.
All eirdlie Joy and mirth I set areir.
Allace this day, allace this wofull tyde,
Quhen I began with my Goddis for to Chyde.'

Be this was said ane Chyld come fra the Hall
To warn Cresseid the Supper was reddy,
First knokkit at the dure, and syne culd call: 360
'Madame your Father biddis yow cum in hy.
He hes mervell sa lang on grouf ye ly,
And sayis your prayers bene to lang sum deill:
The goddis wait all your Intent full weill.'

Quod scho: 'Fair Chyld ga to my Father deir,
And pray him cum to speik with me anone.'
And sa he did, and said: 'douchter quhat cheir?'
'Allace' (quod scho), 'Father my mirth is gone.'
'How sa' (quod he); and scho can all expone
As I have tauld, the vengeance and the wraik   370
For hir trespas, Cupide on hir culd tak.

He luikit on hir uglye Lipper face,
The quhilk befor was quhyte as Lillie flour,
Wringand his handis oftymes he said allace
That he had levit to se that wofull hour,
For he knew weill that thair was na succour
To hir seiknes, and that dowblit his pane.
Thus was thair cair aneuch betuix thame twane.

Quhen thay togidder murnit had full lang,
Quod Cresseid: 'Father, I wald not be kend.   380
Thairfoir in secreit wyse ye let me gang
Into yone Hospitall at the tounis end.
And thidder sum meit for Cheritie me send
To leif upon, for all mirth in this eird
Is fra me gane, sic is my wickit weird.'

Than in ane Mantill and ane bawer Hat,
With Cop and Clapper wonder prively,
He opnit ane secreit yet, and out thair at
Convoyit hir, that na man suld espy,
Into ane Village half ane myle thairby,   390
Delyverit hir in at the Spittaill hous,
And daylie sent hir part of his Almous.

Sum knew her weill, & sum had na knawledge
Of hir becaus scho was sa deformait,
With bylis blak ouirspred in hir visage,
And hir fair colour faidit and alterait.
Yit thay presumit for her hie regrait
And still murning, scho was of Nobill kin:
With better will thairfoir they tuik hir in.

The day passit, and Phebus went to rest,   400
The Cloudis blak ouirquhelmit all the sky.
God wait gif Cresseid was ane sorrowfull Gest,

56

Seing that uncouth fair and Harbery:
But meit or drink scho dressit hir to ly
In ane dark Corner of the Hous allone.
And on this wyse weiping. scho maid her mone:

THE COMPLAINT OF CRESSEID

'O sop of sorrow, sonkin into cair:
O Cative Creisseid, for now and ever mair,
Gane is thy Joy and all thy mirth in Eird,
Of all blyithnes now art thou blaiknit bair.   **410**
Thair is na Salve my saif the of thy sair,
Fell is thy Fortoun, wickit is thy weird:
Thy blys is baneist, and thy baill on breird,
Under the Eirth, God gif I gravin wer:
Quhair nane of Grece nor yit of Troy micht heird.

'Quhair is thy Chalmer wantounlie besene?
With burely bed and bankouris browderit bene,
Spycis and Wyne to thy Collatioun,
The Cowpis all of gold and silver schene:
The sweit Meitis, servit in plaittis clene,   **420**
With Saipheron sals of ane gud sessoun:
Thy gay garmentis with mony gudely Goun,
Thy plesand Lawn pinnit with goldin prene:
All is areir, they greit Royall Renoun.

'Quhair is thy garding with thir greissis gay?
And fresche flowris, quhilk the Quene Floray
Had paintit plesandly in ererie pane,
Quhair thou was wont full merilye in May,
To walk and tak the dew be it was day
And heir the Merle and Mawis mony ane,   **430**

With Ladyis fair in Carrolling to gane,
And se the Royall Rinkis in thair array,
In garmentis gay garnischit on everie grane.

'Thy greit triumphand fame and hie honour,
Quhair thou was callit of Eirdlye wichtis Flour,
All is decayit, thy weird is welterit so.
Thy hie estait is turnit in darknes dour.
This Lipper Ludge tak for they burelie Bour.
And for thy Bed tak now ane bunche of stro,
For waillit Wyne, and Meitis thou had tho,   440
Tak mowlit Breid, Peirrie and Ceder sour:
Bot Cop and Clapper, now is all ago.

'My cleir voice, and courtlie carrolling,
Quhair I was wont with Ladyis for to sing,
Is rawk as Ruik, full hiddeous hoir and hace,
My plesand port all utheris precelling:
Of lustines I was hald maist conding.
Now is deformit the Figour of my face,
To luik on it, na Leid now lyking hes:
Sowpit in syte, I say with sair siching,   450
Ludgeit amang the Lipper Leid allace.

'O Ladyis fair of Troy and Grece, attend
My miserie, quhilk nane may comprehend.
My frivoll Fortoun, my Infelicitie:
My greit mischeif quhilk na man can amend.
Be war in tyme, approchis neir the end,
And in your mynd ane mirrour mak of me:
As I am now, peradventure that ye
For all your micht may cum to that same end,
Or ellis war, gif ony war may be.   460

'Nocht is your fairnes bot ane faiding flour,
Nocht is your famous laud and hie honour

Bot wind Inflat in uther mennis eiris.
Your roising reid to rotting sall retour:
Exempill mak of me in your Memour,
Quhilk of sic thingis wofull witness beiris,
All Welth in Eird, away as Wind it weiris.
Be war thairfoir, approchis neir the hour:
Fortoun is fikkill, quhen scho beginnis & steiris.'

Thus chydand with hir drerie destenye,   470
Weiping, scho woik the nicht fra end to end.
Bot all in vane; hir dule, hir cairfull cry
Micht not remeid, nor yit hir murning mend.
Ane Lipper Lady rais and till hir wend,
And said: 'quhy spurnis thow aganis the Wall,
To sla thy self, and mend nathing at all?

'Sen thy weiping dowbillis bot thy wo,
I counsall the mak vertew of ane neid.
To leir to clap thy Clapper to and fro,
And leir efter the Law of Lipper Leid.'   480
Thair was na buit, bot furth with thame scho yeid,
Fra place to place, quhill cauld and hounger sair
Compellit hir to be ane rank beggair.

That samin tyme of Troy the Garnisoun,
Quhilk had to chiftane worthie Troylus,
Throw Jeopardie of Weir had strikken doun
Knichtis of Grece in number mervellous,
With greit tryumphe and Laude victorious
Agane to Troy [richt] Royallie they raid
The way quhair Cresseid with the Lipper baid.   490

Seeing that companie thai come all with ane stevin
Thay gaif ane cry and schuik coppis gude speid.
Said 'worthie Lordis for goddis lufe of Hevin,

To us Lipper part of your Almous deid.'
Than to thair cry Nobill Troylus tuik heid,
Having pietie, neir by the place can pas:
Quhair Cresseid sat, not witting quhat scho was.

Than upon him scho kest up baith hir Ene,
And with ane blenk it come into his thocht,
That he sumtime hir face befoir had sene,   500
Bot scho was in sic plye he knew hir nocht;
Yit than hir luik into his mynd it brocht
The sweit visage and amorous blenking
Of fair Cresseid sumtyme his awin darling.

Na wonder was, suppois in mynd that he
Tuik hir figure sa sone, and lo now quhy?
The Idole of ane thing, in cace may be
Sa deip Imprentit in the fantasy
That it deludis the wittis outwardly,
And sa appeiris in forme and lyke estait,   510
Within the mynd as it was figurait.

Ane spark of lufe than till his hart culd spring
And kendlit all his bodie in ane fyre.
With hait Fewir ane sweit and trimbling
Him tuik, quhill he was reddie to expyre.
To beir his Scheild, his Breist began to tyre
Within ane quhyle he changit mony hew,
And nevertheless not ane ane uther knew.

For Knichtlie pietie and memoriall
Of fair Cresseid, ane Gyrdill can he tak,   520
Ane Purs of gold, and mony gay Jowall,
And in the Skirt of Cresseid doun can swak;
Than raid away, and not ane word [he] spak,
Pensive in hart, quhill he come to the Toun,
And for greit care oft syis almaist fell doun.

The lipper folk to Cresseid than can draw,
To se the equall distributioun
Of the Almous, bot quhen the gold thay saw,
Ilk ane to uther prevelie can roun,
And said: 'Yone Lord hes mair affectioun,   530
How ever it be, unto yone Lazarous
Than to us all, we knaw be his Almous.'

'Quhat Lord is yone' (quod scho), 'have ye na feill,
Hes done to us so greit humanitie?'
'Yes' (quod a Lipper man), 'I knaw him weill,
Schir Troylus it is, gentill and fre':
Quhen Cresseid understude that it was he,
Stiffer than steill, thair stert ane bitter stound
Throwout hir hart, and fell doun to the ground.

Quhen scho ouircome, with siching sair & sad,   540
With mony cairfull cry and cald ochane:
'Now is my breist with stormie stoundis stad,
Wrappit in wo, ane wretch full will of wane.'
Than swounit scho oft or scho culd refrane,
And ever in hir swouning cryit scho thus:
'O fals Cresseid and trew Knicht Troylus.

'Thy lufe, thy lawtie, and they gentilnes,
I countit small in my prosperitie,
Sa elevait I was in wantones,
And clam upon the fickill quheill sa hie: 550
All Faith and Lufe I promissit to the,
Was in the self fickill and frivolous:
O fals Cresseid, and trew Knicht Troilus.

'For lufe, of me thou keipt gude continence,
Honest and chaist in conversatioun.
Of all wemen protectour and defence

61

Thou was, and helpit thair opinioun.
My mynd in fleschelie foull affectioun
Was Inclynit to Lustis Lecherous:
Fy fals Cresseid, O trew Knicht Troylus.   560

'Lovers be war and tak gude heid about
Quhome that ye lufe, for quhome ye suffer paine.
I lat yow wit, thair is richt few thairout
Quhome ye may traist to have trew lufe agane.
Preif quhen ye will, your labour is in vaine.
Thairfoir, I reid, ye tak thame as ye find,
For thay ar sad as Widdercock in Wind,

'Becaus I knaw the greit unstabilnes
Brukkill as glas, into my self I say,
Traisting in uther als greit unfaithfulnes: 570
Als unconstant, and als untrew of fay.
Thocht sum be trew, I wait richt few ar thay,
Quha findis treuth lat him his Lady ruse:
Nane but my self as now I will accuse.'

Quhen this was said, with Paper scho sat doun,
And on this maneir maid hir Testament.
'Heir I beteiche my Corps and Carioun
With Wormis and with Taidis to be rent.
My Cop and Clapper and myne Ornament,
And all my gold the Lipper folk sall have,   580
Quhen I am deid, to burie me in grave.

'This Royal Ring, set with this Rubie reid,
Quhilk Troylus in drowrie to me send,
To him agane I leif it quhen I am deid,
To mak my cairfull deid unto him kend:
Thus I conclude schortlie and mak ane end,
My Spreit I leif to Diane quhair scho dwellis,
To walk with hir in waist Woddis and Wellis.

'O Diomeid, thou hes baith Broche and Belt,
Quhilk Troylus gave me in takning   590
Of his trew lufe,' and with that word scho swelt.
And sone ane Lipper man tuik of the Ring,
Syne buryit hir withouttin tarying:
To Troylus furthwith the Ring he bair,
And of Cresseid the deith he can declair.

Quhen he had hard hir greit infirmitie,
Hir Legacie and Lamentatioun,
And how scho endit in sic povertie,
He swelt for wo, and fell doun in ane swoun,
For greit sorrow his hart to brist was boun: 600
Siching full sadlie, said: 'I can no moir,
Scho was untrew, and wo is me thairfoir.'

Sum said he maid ane Tomb of Merbell gray,
And wrait hir name and superscriptioun,
And laid it on hir grave quhair that scho lay,
In goldin Letteris, conteining this ressoun:
'Lo, fair Laydis, Crisseid, of Troyis toun,
Sumtyme countit the flour of Womanheid,
Under this stane lait Lipper lyis deid.'

Now, worthie Wemen, in this Ballet schort,   610
Made for your worschip and Instructioun,
Of Cheritie, I monische and exhort,
Ming not your lufe with fals deceptioun.
Beir in your mynd this schort conclusioun
Of fair Cresseid, as I have said befoir.
Sen scho is deid, I speik of hir no moir.

Finis.

(Wood, *Poems and Fables of Henryson*)

Allone as I went up and doun
in ane abbay was fair to se,
Thinkand quhat consolatioun
Was best in to adversitie,
On caiss I kest on syd myne E,
And saw this writtin upoun a wall:
'off quhat estait, man, that thow be,
Obey and thank thy god of all.

'Thy kyndome and thy grit empyre,
Thy ryaltie, nor riche array,   10
Sall nocht endeur at thy desyre,
Bot as the wind will wend away;
Thy gold and all thy gudis gay,
quhen fortoun list will fra the fall;
Sen thow sic sampillis seis ilk day,
Obey and thank thy god of all.

'Job wes maist riche in writ we find,
Thobe maist full of cheritie:
Job woux pure, and thobe blynd,
Bath tempit with adversitie.   20
Sen blindness wes infirmitie,
and poverty wes naturall,
Thairfoir rycht patiently bath he and he
Obeyid and thankit god of all.

'Thocht thow be blind, or haif ane halt,
Or in thy face deformit ill,
Sa it cum nocht throw thy defalt,
Na man suld the repreif by skill.

Blame nocht thy Lord, sa is his will;
Spurn nocht thy fute aganis the wall;   30
Bot with meik hairt and prayer still
obey and thank thy god of all.

'God of his justice mon correct,
and of his mercy petie haif;
he is ane Juge to nane suspect,
To puneiss synfull man and saif.
Thocht thow be lord attour the laif,
and eftirwart maid bound and thrall,
ane pure begger, with skrip and staif,
obey and thank thy god of all.   40

'This changeing and grit variance
off erdly staitis up and doun
Is nocht bot causualitie and chance,
as sum men sayis, without ressoun,
Bot be the grit provisioun
of god aboif that rewll the sall;
Thairfoir evir thow mak the boun
To obey and thank thy god of all.

'In welth be meik, heich nocht thy self;
be glaid in wilfull povertie;   50
Thy power and thy warldis pelf
Is nocht bot verry vanitie.
Remember him that deit on tre,
For thy saik taistit the bittir gall;
quha heis law hairtis and lawis he;
obey and thank thy god of all.'

Finis: quod mr ro^{t} henrysone.

(*Bannatyne MS*, Wood, *Poems and Fables*)

[Robene and Makyne]

Robene sat on gud grene hill,
Kepand a flok of fe:
mirry makyne said him till,
'Robene, thou rew on me;
I haif the luvit lowd and still
Thir yeiris two or thre;
my dule in dern bot gif thow dill,
Dowtless but dreid I de.'

Robene ansert, 'be the rude,
nathing of lufe I knaw,
Bot keipis my scheip undir yone wid,
Lo quhair thay raik on raw:
quhat hes marrit the in thy mude,
makyne, to me thow schaw;
Or quhat is lufe, or to be lude?
Fane wald I leir that law.'

'At luvis lair gife thow will leir,
Tak thair ane a b c:
be heynd, courtass, and fair of feir,
Wyse, hardy and fre;
So that no denger do the deir,
quhat dule in dern thow dre;
preiss the with pane at all poweir,
be patient and previe.'

Robene anserit hir agane,
'I wait not quhat is luve;
Bot I haif mervell incertane
Quhat makis the this wanrufe:

66

The weddir is fair, & I am fane,
my scheip gois haill aboif;   30
And we wald play us in this plane,
They wald us bayth reproif.'

'Robene, tak tent unto my taill,
And wirk all as I reid,
And thow sall haif my hairt all haill,
Eik and my madinheid.
Sen god sendis bute for baill,
And for murning remeid,
In dern with the, bot gif I daill,
Dowtles I am bot deid.'   40

'Makyne, to morne this ilk a tyde,
And ye will meit me heir,
Peraventure my scheip ma gang besyd,
quhill we haif liggit full neir;
Bot mawgre haif I and I byd
Fra thay begin to steir;
quhat lyis on hairt I will not hyd;
Makyn, than mak gud cheir.'

'Robene, thow reivis me roif and rest;
I luve bot the allone.'   50
'Makyne, adew, the sone gois west,
The day is neir hand gone.'
'Robene, in dule I am so drest,
That lufe wilbe my bone.'
'Ga lufe, makyne, quhair evir thow list,
ffor lemman I (bid) none.'

'Robene, I stand in sic a styll;
I sicht, and that full sair.'
'Makyne, I haif bene heir this quhyle;
at hame god gif I wair.'   60

'my huny, robene, talk ane quhill,
gif thow will do na mair.'
'Makyne, sum uthir man begyle,
ffor hamewart I will fair.'

Robene on his wayis went,
als licht as leif of tre;
mawkin murnit in hir intent,
and trowd him nevir to se.
Robene brayd attour the bent;
Than mawkyne cryit on hie,   70
'Now ma thow sing, for I am schent!
quhat alis lufe at me?'

Mawkyne went hame withowttin faill,
Full wery eftir cowth weip:
Than robene in a fulfair daill
Assemblit all his scheip.
Be that sum pairte of mawkynis aill
Outthrow his hairt cowd creip;
he fallowit hir fast thair till assaill,
and till hir tuke gude keip.   80

'Abyd, abyd, thow fair makyne,
a word for ony thing;
For all my luve it salbe thyne,
Withowttin depairting.
all haill, thy harte for till haif myne
Is all my cuvating;
my scheip to morne quhill houris nyne
Will neid of no keping.'

'Robene, thow hes hard soung & say,
In gestis and storeis auld,   90
The man that will nocht quhen he may
Sall haif nocht quhen he wald.

68

I pray to Jesu every day
mot eik thair Cairis cauld,
that first preiss with the to play,
be firth, forrest, or fawld.'

'Makyne, the nicht is soft and dry,
The wedder is warme & fair,
And the grene woid rycht neir us by
To walk attour all quhair;   100
Thair ma na Janglour us espy,
That is to lufe contrair;
Thairin, makyne, bath ye & I
Unsene we ma repair.'

'Robene, that warld is all away
and quhyt brocht till ane end,
and nevir agane thairto perfay
Sall it be as thow wend;
For of my pane thow maid it play,
and all in vane I spend;   110
as thow hes done, so sall I say,
murne on, I think to mend.'

'Mawkyne, the howp of all my heill,
my hairt on the is sett,
and evirmair to the be leill,
quhill I may leif but lett;
nevir to faill, as utheris feill,
quhat grace that evir I gett.'
'Robene, with the I will nocht deill;
Adew, for thus we mett.'   120

Malkyne went hame blyth annewche,
Attour the holttis hair;
Robene murnit, and Malkyne lewche,
Scho sang, he sichit sair;

69

and so left him, bayth wo & wrewche,
In dolour & in cair,
Kepand his hird under a huche,
amangis the holtis hair.

(*Bannatyne MS*, Wood, *Poems and Fables*)

[*The Prais of Aige*]

Wythin a garth, under a rede rosere,
Ane ald man, and decrepit, herd I syng;
Gay was the note, suete was the voce et clere:
It was grete joy to here of sik a thing.
'And to my dome', he said, in his dyting,
'For to be yong I wald not, for my wis
Off all this warld to mak me lord et king.
The more of age the nerar hevynnis blis.

'False is this warld, and full of variance,
Besoucht with syn and other sytis mo;   10
Treuth is all tynt, gyle has the gouvernance,
Wrechitnes has wroht all welthis wele to wo;
Fredome is tynt, and flemyt the lordis fro,
And covatise is all the cause of this;
I am content that youthede is ago:
The more of age the nerar hevynnis blisse.

'The state of youth I repute for na gude,
For in that state sik perilis now I see;
Bot full smal grace, the regeing of his blude
Can none gaynstand quhill that he agit be;   20
Syne of the thing that tofore joyit he
Nothing remaynis for to be callit his;
For quhy it were bot very vanitee:
The more of age the nerar hevynnis blisse.

'Suld no man traist this wrechit warld, for quhy
Of erdly joy ay sorow is the end;
The state of it can noman certify,
This day a king, to morne na gude to spend.
Quhat have we here bot grace us to defend?
The quhilk god grant us for to mend oure mys,   30
That to his glore he may oure saulis send;
The more of age the nerar hevynnis blisse.'

(ffinis: quod hendersone) Chepman & Myllar 1508.

(Wood, *Poems and Fables*)

The Taill of the Foxe, that begylit the Wolf, in the schadow of the Mone

In elderis dayis, as Esope can declair,
Thair wes ane Husband, quhilk had ane pleuch to steir.
His use wes ay in morning to ryse air;
Sa happinnit him in streiking tyme off yeir
Airlie in the morning to follow ffurth his feir,
Unto the pleuch, bot his gadman and he;
His stottis he straucht with 'Benedicite.'

The Caller cryit: 'how, haik, upon hicht;
Hald draucht, my dowis;' syne broddit thame ffull sair.
The Oxin wes unusit, young and licht,   10
And ffor fersnes thay couth the fur fforfair.
The Husband than woxe angrie as ane hair,
Syne cryit, and caist his Patill and grit stanis:
'The Wolff' (quod he) 'mot have yow all at anis.'

Bot yit the Wolff wes neirar nor he wend,
For in ane busk he lay, and Lowrence baith,

71

In ane Rouch Rone, wes at the furris end,
And hard the hecht; than Lowrence leuch full raith:
'To tak yone bud' (quod he) 'it were na skaith.'
'Weill' (quod the Wolff), 'I hecht the be my hand;   20
Yone Carllis word, as he wer King, sall stand.'

The Oxin waxit mair reullie at the last;
Syne efter thay lousit, ffra that it worthit weill lait;
The Husband hamewart with his cattell past.
Than sone the Wolff come hirpilland in his gait,
Befoir the Oxin, and schupe to mak debait.
The Husband saw him, and worthit sumdeill agast,
And bakwart with his beistis wald haif past.

The Wolff said, 'quhether dryvis thou this Pray?
I chalenge it, ffor nane off thame ar thyne.'   30
The man thairoff wes in ane felloun fray,
And soberlie to the Wolff answerit syne:
'Schir, be my Saull, thir oxin ar all myne;
Thairfoir I studdie quhy ye suld stop me,
Sen that I faltit never to you, trewlie.'

The Wolff said, 'Carle, gaif thou not me this drift
Airlie, quhen thou wes eirrand on yone bank?
And is thair oucht (sayis thou) frear than gift?
This tarying wyll tyne the all thy thank;
Far better is frelie ffor to giff ane plank   40
Nor be compellit on force to giff ane mart.
Fy on the fredome that cummis not with hart!'

'Schir' (quod the husband), 'ane man may say in greif,
And syne ganesay, fra he avise and se:
I hecht to steill, am I thairfoir ane theif?'
'God forbid, Schir, all hechtis suld haldin be!'
'Gaif I my hand or oblissing' (quod he),

'Or have ye witnes, or writ ffor to schaw?
Schir, reif me not, but go and seik the Law!'

'Carll' (quod the Wolff), 'ane Lord, and he be leill,   50
That schrinkis for schame, or doutis to be repruvit,
His saw is ay als sickker as his Seill.
Fy on the Leid that is not leill and lufit!
Thy argument is fals, and eik contrufit,
For it is said in Proverb: "But lawte
All uther vertewis ar nocht worth ane fle." '

'Schir,' said the husband, 'remember of this thing:
Ane leill man is not tane at halff ane taill.
I may say, and ganesay, I am na King:
Quhair is your witnes that hard I hecht thame haill?'   60
Than said the Wolff, 'thairfoir it sall nocht faill;
Lowrence' (quod he), 'cum hidder of that Schaw,
And say na thing bot as thow hard and saw.'

Lowrence come lourand, for he lufit never licht,
And sone appeirit befoir thame in that place:
The man leuch na thing, quhen he saw that sicht.
'Lowrence' (quod the Wolff), 'Thow man declair this cace,
Quhairof we sall schaw the suith in schort space;
I callit on the leill witnes for to beir:
Quhat hard thow that this man hecht me lang eir?'   70

'Schir' (said the Tod), 'I can not hastelie
Swa sone as now gif sentence finall;
Bot wald ye baith submit yow heir to me,
To stand at my decreit perpetuall,
To pleis baith I suld preif, gif it may fall.'
'Weill' (quod the Wolff), 'I am content for me:'
The man said, 'swa am I, how ever it be.'

Than schew thay furth thair allegeance but fabill,
And baith proponit thair pley to him compleit.
(Quod Lowrence): 'now I am ane Juge amycabill: 80
Ye sall be sworne to stand at my decreit,
Quhether heirefter ye think it soure or sweit.'
The Wolff braid furth his fute, the man his hand,
And on the Toddis Taill sworne thay ar to stand.

Than tuke the Tod the man furth till ane syde,
And said him, 'friend, thow art in blunder brocht;
The Wolff will not forgif the ane Oxe hyde,
Yit wald my self fane help the, and I mocht;
Bot I am laith to hurt my conscience ocht.
Tyne nocht thy querrell in thy awin defence;   90
This will not throw but grit coist and expence.

'Seis thow not Buddis beiris Bernis throw,
And giftis garris crukit materis hald ffull evin?
Sumtymis ane hen haldis ane man in ane Kow.
All ar not halie that heifis thair handis to hevin.'
'Schir' (said the man), 'ye sall have sex or sevin,
Richt off the fattest hennis off all the floik:
I compt not all the laif, leif me the Coik.'

'I am ane Juge' (quod Lowrence than), and leuch;
'Thair is na Buddis suld beir me by the rycht;   100
I may tak hennis and Caponis weill aneuch,
For God is gane to sleip; as ffor this nycht,
Sic small thingis ar not sene in to his sicht;
Thir hennis' (quod he) 'sall mak thy querrell sure,
With emptie hand na man suld Halkis lure.'

Concordit thus, than Lowrence tuke his leiff,
And to the Wolff he went in to ane ling;
Syne prevelie he plukkit him be the sleiff:

'Is this in ernist' (quod he) 'ye ask sic thing?
Na, be my Saull, I trow it be in heithing.'   110
Than saith the Wolff, 'Lowrence, quhy sayis thow sa?
Thow hard the hecht thy selff that he couth ma.'

'The hecht' (quod he) 'yone man maid at the pleuch,
Is that the cause quhy ye the cattell craif?'
Halff in to heithing (said Lowrence than), and leuch;
'Schir, be the Rude, unroikit now ye raif;
The Devill ane stirk taill thairfoir sall ye haif;
Wald I tak it upon my conscience
To do sa pure ane man as yone offence?

'Yit haif I communit with the Carll' (quod he);   120
'We ar concordit upon this cunnand:
Quyte off all clamis, swa ye will mak him fre,
Ye sall ane Cabok have in to your hand,
That sic ane sall not be in all this land;
For it is Somer Cheis, baith fresche and ffair;
He sayis it weyis ane stane, and sumdeill mair.'

'Is that thy counsell' (quod the Wolff), 'I do,
That yone Carll ffor ane Cabok suld be fre?'
'Ye, be my Saull, and I were sworne yow to,
Ye suld nane uther counsell have for me;   130
For gang ye to the maist extremitie,
It will not wyn yow worth ane widderit neip;
Schir, trow ye not, I have ane Saull to keip?'

'Weill' (quod the Wolff), 'it is aganis my will
That yone Carll for ane Cabok suld ga quyte.'
'Schir' (quod the Tod), 'ye tak it in nane evill,
For, be my Saull, your self had all the wyte.'
'Than' (said the Wolff) 'I bid na mair to flyte,
Bot I wald se yone Cabok off sic pryis.'
'Schir' (said the Tod), 'he tauld me quhar it lyis.'   140

Than hand in hand thay held unto ane hill;
The Husband till his hors hes tane the way,
For he wes fane; he schaipit ffrom thair ill,
And on his feit woke the dure quhill day.
Now will we turne vnto the other tway.
Throw woddis waist thir Freikis on fute can fair,
Fra busk to busk, quhill neir midnycht and mair.

Lowrence wes ever remembring upon wrinkis
And subtelteis the Wolff for to begyle;
That he had hecht ane Caboik, he forthinkis,   150
Yit at the last he findis furth ane wyle,
Than at him self softlie couth he smyle.
The Wolff sayis, 'Lowrence, thow playis bellie blind;
We seik all nycht, bot na thing can we find.'

'Schir' (said the Tod), 'we ar at it almaist;
Soft yow ane lytill, and ye sall se it sone.'
Than to ane Manure place thay hyit in haist;
The nicht wes lycht, and pennyfull the Mone.
Than till ane draw well thir Senyeours past but hone,
Quhair that twa bukkettis severall suithlie hang;   160
As ane come up, ane uther doun wald gang.

The schadow of the Mone schone in the well.
'Schir' (said Lowrence), 'anis ye sall find me leill;
Now se ye not the Caboik weill your sell,
Quhyte as ane Neip, and round als as ane seill?
He hang it yonder, that na man suld it steill:
Schir, traist ye weill, yone Caboik ye se hing
Micht be ane present to ony Lord or King.'

'Na' (quod the Wolff) 'mycht I yone Caboik haif
On the dry land, as I it yonder se,   170
I wald quitclame the Carll of all the laif;

76

His dart Oxin I compt thame not ane fle;
Yone wer mair meit for sic ane man as me.
Lowrence' (quod he), 'leip in the bukket sone,
And I sall hald the ane, quhill thow have done.'

Lowrence gird doun baith sone and subtellie;
The uther baid abufe, and held the flaill.
'It is sa mekill' (quod Lowrence) 'it maisteris me,
On all my tais it hes not left ane naill;
Ye man mak help upwart, and it haill   180
Leip in the uther bukket haistelie,
And cum sone doun, and make me sum supple.'

Than lychtlie in the bukket lap the loun;
His wecht but weir the uther end gart ryis;
The Tod come hailland up, the Wolf yeid doun;
Than angerlie the Wolff upon him cryis:
'I cummand thus dounwart, quhy thow upwart hyis?'
'Schir' (quod the Foxe), 'thus fairis it off Fortoun:
As ane cummis up, scho quheillis ane uther doun!'

Than to the ground sone yeid the Wolff in haist;   190
The Tod lap on land, als blyith as ony bell,
And left the Wolff in watter to the waist.
Quha haillit him out, I wait not, off the well.
Heir endis the Text; thair is na mair to tell.
Yit men may find ane gude moralitie
In this sentence, thocht it ane Fabill be.

Moralitas

This Wolff I likkin to ane wickit man,
Quhilk dois the pure oppres in everie place,
And pykis at thame all querrellis that he can,

77

Be Rigour, reif, and uther wickitnes. 200
The Foxe and the Feind I call in to this cais,
Actand ilk man to ryn unrychteous rinkis,
Thinkand thairthrow to lok him in his linkis.

The Husband may be callit ane godlie man,
With quhome the Feynd falt findes (as Clerkis reids),
Besie to tempt him with all wayis that he can.
The hennis ar warkis that fra ferme faith proceidis:
Quhair sic sproutis spreidis, the evill spreit thair not speids,
Bot wendis vnto the wickit man agane;
That he hes tint his travell is full unfane. 210

The wodds waist, quhairin wes the Wolff wyld,
Ar wickit riches, quhilk all men gaipis to get;
Quha traistis in sic Trusterie ar oft begyld;
For Mammon may be callit the Devillis Net,
Quhilk Sathanas for all sinfull hes set.
With proud plesour quha settis his traist thairin,
But speciall grace, lychtlie can not outwin.

The Cabok may be callit Covetyce,
Quhilk blomis braid in mony mannis Ee;
Wa worth the well of that wickit vyce! 220
For it is all bot fraud and fantasie,
Dryvand ilk man to leip in the buttrie
That dounwart drawis unto the pane of hell.
Christ keip all Christianis from that wickit well!

Finis

(Wood, *Poems and Fables*)

WALTER KENNEDY

Honour with Age

At matyne houre in midis of the nicht,
Walknit of sleip I saw besyd me sone
Ane aigit man semit sextie yeiris of sicht
This sentence sett and song it in gud tone:
'Omnipotent and eterne God in trone,
To be content and lufe the I haif caus
That my licht yowtheid is opprest and done;
Honor with age to every vertew drawis.

Grene yowth, to aige thow mon obey and bow;
Thy foly lustis lestis skant ane May;   10
That than wes witt, is naturall foly now,
As warldly witt, honor, riches or fresche array;
Deffy the devill; dreid God and domisday,
For all salbe accusit as thow knawis;
Blissit be God my yutheid is away;
Honor with aige to every vertew drawis.

O bittir yowith that semis delitious;
O haly aige that sumtyme semit soure;
O restles yowth hie, hait, and vicious;
O honest aige fulfillit with honoure;   20
O frawart yowth, frutles and fedand flour,
Contrair to conscience baith to God and lawis,
Off all vanegloir the lamp and the mirroure;
Honor with aige till every vertew drawis

This warld is sett for to dissaive us evin;
Pryd is the nett and covece is the trane;
For na reward except the joy of hevin
Wald I be yung in to this warld agane;
The schip of faith tempestous wind and rane
Dryvis in the see of Lollerdry that blawis: 30
My yowth is gane and I am glaid and fane;
Honor with aige till every vertew drawis.

Law, luve and lawtie gravin law thay ly;
Dissimulance hes borrowit conscience clayis;
Aithis, writ, walx nor seilis ar not set by;
Flattery is fosterit baith with freindis and fayis;
The sone to bruike it that his fader hais
Wald se him deid, Sathanas sic seid sawis;
Yowtheid adew, ane of my mortall fais;
Honor with aige with every vertew drawis.   40

ffinis q kennedy

(*Bannatyne MS*, II)

WILLIAM DUNBAR

The Goldyn Targe

Ryght as the stern of day begouth to schyne,
Quhen gone to bed war Vesper and Lucyne,
  I raise and by a rosere did me rest;
Up sprang the goldyn candill matutyne,
With clere depurit bemes cristallyne,
  Glading the mery foulis in thair nest;
  Or Phebus was in purpur cape revest
Up raise the lark, the hevyns menstrale fyne
  In May, in till a morow myrthfullest.

Full angellike thir birdis sang thair houris   10
Within thair courtyns grene, in to thair bouris
  Apparalit quhite and red wyth blomes suete;
Anamalit was the felde wyth all colouris,
The perly droppis schake in silvir schouris,
  Quhill all in balme did branch and levis flete;
  To part fra Phebus did Aurora grete,
Hir cristall teris I saw hyng on the flouris,
  Quhilk he for lufe all drank up wyth his hete.

For mirth of May, wyth skippis and wyth hoppis.
The birdis sang upon the tender croppis,   20
  With curiouse note, as Venus chapell clerkis:
The rosis yong, new spreding of thair knopis,
War powderit brycht with hevinly beriall droppis,
  Throu bemes rede birnyng as ruby sperkis;
  The skyes rang for schoutyng of the larkis,

The purpur hevyn, our scailit in silvir sloppis,
　Ourgilt the treis, branchis, lef, and barkis.

Doune throu the ryce a ryvir ran wyth stremys,
So lustily agayn thai lykand lemys,
　That all the lake as lamp did leme of licht,　　　　30
Quhilk schadowit all about wyth twynkling glemis;
That bewis bathit war in secund bemys
　Throu the reflex of Phebus visage brycht;
　On every syde the hegies raise on hicht,
The bank was grene, the bruke was full of bremys,
　The stanneris clere as stern in frosty nycht.

The cristall air, the sapher firmament.
The ruby skyes of the orient,
　Kest beriall bemes on emerant bewis grene;
The rosy garth depaynt and redolent,　　　　　　40
With purpur, azure, gold, and goulis gent
　Arayed was, by dame Flora the quene,
　So nobily, that joy was for to sene;
The roch agayn the rivir resplendent
　As low enlumynit all the leves schene.

Quhat throu the mery foulys armony,
And throu the ryveris soune rycht ran me by,
　On Florais mantill I slepit as I lay,
Quhare sone in to my dremes fantasy
I saw approch, agayn the orient sky,　　　　　　50
　A saill, als quhite as blossum upon spray,
　Wyth merse of gold, brycht as the stern of day,
Quhilk tendit to the land full lustily,
　As falcoune swift desyrouse of hir pray.

And hard on burd unto the blomyt medis,
Amang the grene rispis and the redis,

82

Arrivit sche, quhar fro anone thare landis
Ane hundreth ladyes, lusty in to wedis,
Als fresch as flouris that in May up spredis,
    In kirtillis grene, withoutyn kell or bandis: 60
    Thair brycht hairis hang gletering on the strandis
In tressis clere, wyppit wyth goldyn thredis;
    With pappis quhite, and mydlis small as wandis.

Discrive I wald, bot quho coud wele endyte
How all the feldis wyth thai lilies quhite
    Depaynt war brycht, quhilk to the hevyn did glete:
Noucht thou, Omer, als fair as thou coud wryte,
For all thine ornate stilis so perfyte;
    Nor yit thou, Tullius, quhois lippis suete
    Off rethorike did in to termes flete: 70
Your aureate tongis both bene all to lyte,
    For to compile that paradise complete.

Thare saw I Nature and Venus, quene and quene,
The fresch Aurora, and lady Flora schene,
    Juno, Appollo, and Proserpyna,
Dyane the goddesse chaste of woddis grene,
My lady Cleo, that help of makaris bene,
    Thetes, Pallas, and prudent Minerva,
    Fair feynit Fortune, and lemand Lucina,
Thir mychti quenis in crounis mycht be sene,   80
    Wyth bemys blith, bricht as Lucifera.

There saw I May, of myrthfull monethis quene,
Betuix Aprile and June, her sistir schene,
    Within the gardyng walking up and doun,
Quham of the foulis gladdith al bedene;
Scho was full tender in hir yeris grene.
    Thare saw I Nature present hir a goune
    Rich to behald and nobil of renoune,

83

Off eviry hew under the hevin that bene
　　Depaynt, and broud be gude proporcioun.　　90

Full lustily thir ladyes all in fere
Enterit within this park of most plesere,
　　Quhare that I lay our helit wyth levis ronk;
The mery foulis, blisfullest of chere,
Salust Nature, me thoucht, on thair manere,
　　And eviry blome on branch, and eke on bonk,
　　Opynt and spred thair balmy levis donk,
Full low enclynyng to thair Quene so clere,
　　Quham of thair nobill norising thay thonk.

Syne to dame Flora, on the samyn wyse,　　100
Thay saluse, and thay thank a thousand syse;
　　And to dame Venus, lufis mychti quene,
Thay sang ballettis in lufe, as was the gyse,
With amourouse notis lusty to devise,
　　As thay that had lufe in thair hertis grene;
　　Thair hony throtis, opnyt fro the splene,
With werblis suete did perse the hevinly skyes,
　　Quhill loud resownyt the firmament serene.

Ane othir court thare saw I consequent,
Cupide the king, wyth bow in hand ybent,　　110
　　And dredefull arowis grundyn scharp and square;
Thare saw I Mars, the god armypotent,
Aufull and sterne, strong and corpolent;
　　Thare saw I crabbit Saturn ald and haire,
　　His luke was lyke for to perturb the aire;
Thare was Mercurius, wise and eloquent,
　　Of rethorike that fand the flouris faire;

Thare was the god of gardingis, Priapus;
Thare was the god of wildernes, Phanus;

And Janus, god of entree delytable;   120
Thare was the god of fludis, Neptunus;
Thare was the god of wyndis, Eolus,
    With variand luke, rycht lyke a lord unstable;
    Thare was Bacus the gladder of the table;
Thare was Pluto, the elrich incubus,
    In cloke of grene, his court usit no sable.

And eviry one of thir, in grene arayit,
On harp or lute full merily thai playit,
    And sang ballettis with michty notis clere:
Ladyes to dance full sobirly assayit,   130
Endlang the lusty ryvir so thai mayit,
    Thair observance rycht hevynly was to here;
    Than crap I throu the levis, and drew nere,
Quhare that I was rycht sudaynly affrayit,
    All throu a luke, quhilk I have boucht full dere.

And schortly for to speke, be lufis quene
I was aspyit, scho bad hir archearis kene
    Go me arrest; and thay no time delayit;
Than ladyes fair lete fall thair mantillis grene,
With bowis big in tressit hairis schene,   140
    All sudaynly thay had a felde arayit;
    And yit rycht gretly was I noucht affrayit,
The party was so plesand for to sene,
    A wonder lusty bikkir me assayit.

And first of all, with bow in hand ybent,
Come dame Beautee, rycht as scho wald me schent;
    Syne folowit all hir dameselis yfere,
With mony diverse aufull instrument,
Unto the pres, Fair Having wyth hir went,
    Fyne Portrature, Plesance, and lusty Chere.   150
    Than come Resoun, with schelde of gold so clere,

In plate and maille, as Mars armypotent,
   Defendit me that nobil chevallere.

Syne tender Youth come wyth hir virgyns ying,
Grene Innocence, and schamefull Abaising,
   And quaking Drede, wyth humble Obedience;
The Goldyn Targe harmyt thay no thing;
Curage in thame was noucht begonne to spring;
   Full sore thay dred to done a violence:
   Suete Womanhede I saw cum in presence,   160
Of artilye a warld sche did in bring,
   Servit wyth ladyes full of reverence.

Sche led wyth hir Nurture and Lawlynes,
Contenence, Pacience, Gude Fame, and Stedfastnes,
   Discrecioun, Gentrise, and Considerance,
Levefell Company, and Honest Besynes,
Benigne Luke, Mylde Chere, and Sobirnes:
   All thir bure ganyeis to do me grevance;
   But Resoun bure the Targe wyth sik constance,
Thair scharp assayes mycht do no dures   170
   To me, for all thair aufull ordynance.

Unto the pres persewit Hie Degree,
Hir folowit ay Estate, and Dignitee,
   Comparisoun, Honour, and Noble Array,
Will, Wantonnes, Renoun, and Libertee,
Richesse, Fredome, and eke Nobilitee:
   Wit ye thay did thair baner hye display;
   A cloud of arowis as hayle schour lousit thay.
And schot, quhill wastit was thair artilye,
   Syne went abak reboytit of their pray.   180

Quhen Venus had persavit this rebute,
Dissymilance scho bad go mak persute,

At all powere to perse the Goldyn Targe;
And scho, that was of doubilnes the rute,
Askit hir choise of archeris in refute.

Venus the best bad hir go wale at large;
Scho tuke Presence, plicht ankers of the barge,
And Fair Calling, that wele a flayn coud schute,
And Cherising for to complete hir charge.

Dame Hamelynes scho tuke in company,   190
That hardy was and hende in archery,
And broucht dame Beautee to the felde agayn;
With all the choice of Venus chevalry
Thay come and bikkerit unabaisitly:
The schour of arowis rappit on as rayn;
Perilouse Presence, that mony syre has slayne,
The bataill broucht on bordour hard us by,
The salt was all the sarar suth to sayn.

Thik was the schote of grundyn dartis kene;
Bot Resoun, with the Scheld of Gold so schene,   200
Warly defendit quho so evir assayit;
The aufull stoure he manly did sustene,
Quhill Presence kest a pulder in his ene,
And than as drunkyn man he all forvayit:
Quhen he was blynd, the fule wyth hym thay playit,
And banyst hym amang the bewis grene;
That sory sicht me sudaynly affrayit.

Than was I woundit to the deth wele nere,
And yoldyn as a wofull prisonnere
To lady Beautee, in a moment space;   210
Me thoucht scho semyt lustiar of chere,
Efter that Resoun tynt had his eyne clere,
Than of before, and lufliare of face:
Quhy was thou blyndit, Resoun? quhi, allace!

And gert ane hell my paradise appere,
  And mercy seme, quhare that I fand no grace.

Dissymulance was besy me to sile,
And Fair Calling did oft apon me smyle,
  And Cherising me fed wyth wordis fair;
New Acquyntance enbracit me a quhile,   220
And favouryt me, quhill men mycht go a myle,
  Syne tuk hir leve, I saw hir nevir mare:
  Than saw I Dangere toward me repair,
I could eschew hir presence be no wyle.
  On syde scho lukit wyth ane fremyt fare,

And at the last departing coud hir dresse,
And me delyverit unto Hevynesse
  For to remayne, and scho in cure me tuke.
Be this the Lord of Wyndis, wyth wodenes,
God Eolus, his bugill blew I gesse,   230
  That with the blast the levis all to-schuke;
  And sudaynly, in the space of a luke,
All was hyne went, thare was bot wildernes,
  Thare was no more bot birdis, bank, and bruke.

In twynkling of ane eye to schip thai went,
And swyth up saile unto the top thai stent,
  And with swift course atour the flude thay frak;
Thay fyrit gunnis wyth powder violent,
Till that the reke raise to the firmament,
  The rochis all resownyt wyth the rak,   240
  For rede it semyt that the raynbow brak;
Wyth spirit affrayde apon my fete I sprent
  Amang the clewis, so carefull was the crak.

And as I did awake of my sueving,
The joyfull birdis merily did syng

For myrth of Phebus tendir bemes schene;
Suete war the vapouris, soft the morowing,
Halesum the vale, depaynt wyth flouris ying;
  The air attemperit, sobir, and amene;
  In quhite and rede was all the felde besene,   250
Throu Naturis nobil fresch anamalyng,
  In mirthfull May, of eviry moneth Quene.

O reverend Chaucere, rose of rethoris all,
As in oure tong ane flour imperiall,
  That raise in britane evir, quho redis rycht,
Thou beris of makaris the tryumph riall;
Thy fresch anamalit termes celicall
  This mater coud illumynit have full brycht:
  Was thou noucht of oure Inglisch all the lycht,
Surmounting eviry tong terrestriall,   260
  Alls fer as Mayis morow dois mydnycht?

O morall Gower, and Ludgate laureate,
Your sugurit lippis and tongis aureate,
  Bene to oure eris cause of grete delyte;
Your angel mouthis most mellifluate
Oure rude langage has clere illumynate,
  And faire ourgilt oure speche, that imperfyte
  Stude, or your goldyn pennis schupe to wryte;
This Ile before was bare and desolate
  Off rethorike or lusty fresch endyte.   270

Thou lytill Quair, be evir obedient,
Humble, subject, and symple of entent,
  Before the face of eviry connyng wicht:
I knaw quhat thou of rethorike hes spent;
Off all hir lusty rosis redolent
  Is none in to thy gerland sett on hicht;
  Eschame thar of, and draw the out of sicht.

Rude is thy wede, disteynit, bare, and rent,
  Wele aucht thou be aferit of the licht.

(Mackenzie, *Poems of Dunbar*)

In Secreit Place this Hyndir Nycht

In secreit place this hyndir nycht,
I hard ane beyrne say till ane bricht,
'My huny, my hart, my hoip, my heill,
I have bene lang your luifar leill,
And can of yow get confort nane;
How lang will ye with danger deill
Ye brek my hart, my bony ane!'

His bony beird was kemmit and croppit,
Bot all with cale it was bedroppit,
And he wes townysche, peirt, and gukit;   10
He clappit fast, he kist, and chukkit,
As with the glaikis he wer ouirgane;
Yit be his feirris he wald have fukkit;
Ye brek my hart, my bony ane!

Quod he, 'My hairt, sweit as the hunye,
Sen that I borne wes of my mynnye,
I nevir wowit weycht bot yow;
My wambe is of your lufe sa fow,
That as ane gaist I glour and grane,
I trymble sa, ye will not trow;   20
Ye brek my hart, my bony ane!'

'Tehe!' quod scho, and gaif ane gawfe,
'Be still my tuchan and my calfe,
My new spanit howffing fra the sowk,

And all the blythnes of my bowk;
My sweit swanking, saif yow allane
Na leyd I luiffit all this owk;
Fow leis me that graceles gane.'

Quod he, 'My claver, and my curldodie,
My huny soppis, my sweit possodie,   30
Be not oure bosteous to your billie,
Be warme hairtit and not ewill willie;
Your heylis, quhyt as quhalis bane,
Garris ryis on loft my quhillelillie;
Ye brek my hart, my bony ane!'

Quod scho, 'My clype, my unspaynit gyane,
With moderis mylk yit in your mychane,
My belly huddrun, my swete hurle bawsy,
My huny gukkis, my slawsy gawsy,
Your musing waild perse ane harte of stane,   40
Tak gud confort, my grit heidit slawsy,
Fow leis me that graceles gane.'

Quod he, 'My kyd, my capirculyoun,
My bony baib with the ruch brylyoun,
My tendir gyrle, my wallie gowdye,
My tyrlie myrlie, my crowdie mowdie;
Quhone that oure mouthis dois meit at ane,
My stang dois storkyn with your towdie;
Ye brek my hairt, my bony ane!'

Quod scho, 'Now tak me be the hand,   50
Welcum! my golk of Marie land,
My chirrie and my maikles munyoun,
My sowklar sweit as ony unyoun,
My strumill stirk, yit new to spane,
I am applyit to your opunyoun;
I luif rycht weill your graceles gane.'

He gaiff to hir ane apill rubye;
Quod scho, 'Gramercye! my sweit cowhubye.'
And thai twa to ane play began,
Quhilk men dois call the dery dan;   60
Quhill that thair myrthis met baythe in ane.
'Wo is me!' quod scho, 'quhair will ye, man?
Bot now I luif that graceles gane.'

(Mackenzie, *Poems of Dunbar*)

The Tretis of the Tua Mariit Wemen and the Wedo

Apon the Midsummer evin, mirriest of nichtis,
I muvit furth allane, neir as midnicht wes past,
Besyd ane gudlie grein garth, full of gay flouris,
Hegeit, of ane huge hicht, with hawthorne treis;
Quhairon ane bird, on ane bransche, so birst out hir notis
That never ane blythfullar bird was on the beuche hard:
Quhat throw the sugarat sound of hir sang glaid,
And throw the savour sanative of the sueit flouris,
I drew in derne to the dyk to dirkin efter mirthis;
The dew donkit the daill and dynnit the foulis.   10

  I hard, under ane holyn hevinlie grein hewit,
Ane hie speiche, at my hand, with hautand wourdis;
With that in haist to the hege so hard I inthrang
That I was heildit with hawthorne and with heynd leveis:
Throw pykis of the plet thorne I presandlie luikit,
Gif ony persoun wald approche within that plesand garding.

  I saw three gay ladeis sit in ane grene arbeir,
All grathit in to garlandis of fresche gudlie flouris;
So glitterit as the gold wer thair glorius gilt tressis,
Quhill all the gressis did gleme of the glaid hewis;   20

Kemmit was thair cleir hair, and curiouslie sched
Attour thair schulderis doun schyre, schyning full bricht;
With curches, cassin thair abone, of kirsp cleir and thin:
Thair mantillis grein war as the gress that grew in May sessoun,
Fetrit with thair quhyt fingaris about thair fair sydis:
Off ferliful fyne favour war thair faceis meik,
All full of flurist fairheid, as flouris in June;
Quhyt, seimlie, and soft, as the sweit lillies
New upspred upon spray, as new spynist rose;
Arrayit ryallie about with mony rich vardour,   30
That nature full nobillie annamalit with flouris
Off alkin hewis under hevin, that ony heynd knew,
Fragrant, all full of fresche odour fynest of smell.
Ane cumlie tabil coverit wes befoir tha cleir ladeis,
With ryalle cowpis apon rawis full of ryche wynis.
And of thir fair wlonkes, tua weddit war with lordis,
And wes ane wedow, I wis, wantoun of laitis.
And, as thai talk at the tabill of many taill sindry,
Thay wauchitt at the wicht wyne and waris out wourdis;
And syne thai spak more spedelie, and sparit no matiris.   40

    Bewrie, said the Wedo, ye woddit wemen ying,
Quhat mirth ye fand in maryage, sen ye war menis wyffis;
Reveill gif ye rewit that rakles conditioun?
Or gif that ever ye luffit leyd upone lyf mair
Nor thame that ye your fayth hes festinit for ever?
Or gif ye think, had ye chois, that ye wald cheis better?
Think ye it nocht ane blist band that bindis so fast,
That none undo it a deill may bot the deith ane?

    Than spak ane lusty belyf with lustie effeiris;
It, that ye call the blist band that bindis so fast,   50
Is bair of blis, and bailfull, and greit barrat wirkis.
Ye speir, had I fre chois, gif I wald cheis better?
Chenyeis ay ar to eschew; and changeis ar sueit:

93

Sic cursit chance till eschew, had I my chois anis,
Out of the chenyeis of ane churle I chaip suld for evir.
God gif matrimony were made to mell for ane yeir!
It war bot merrens to be mair, bot gif our myndis pleisit:
It is agane the law of luf, of kynd, and of nature,
Togiddir hairtis to strene, that stryveis with uther:
Birdis hes ane better law na bernis be meikill,   60
That ilk yeir, with new joy, joyis ane maik,
And fangis thame ane fresche feyr, unfulyeit, and constant,
And lattis thair fulyeit feiris flie quhair thai pleis.
Cryst gif sic ane consuetude war in this kith haldin!
Than weill war us wemen that evir we war fre;
We suld have feiris as fresche to fang quhen us likit,
And gif all larbaris thair leveis, quhen thai lak curage.
My self suld be full semlie in silkis arrayit,
Gymp, jolie, and gent, richt joyus, and gent [ryce].
I suld at fairis be found new faceis to se;   70
At playis, and at preichingis, and pilgrimages greit,
To schaw my renone, royaly, quhair preis was of folk,
To manifest my makdome to multitude of pepill,
And blaw my bewtie on breid, quhair bernis war mony;
That I micht cheis, and be chosin, and change quhen me lykit.
Than suld I waill ane full weill, our all the wyd realme,
That suld my womanheid weild the lang winter nicht;
And when I gottin had ane grome, ganest of uther,
Yaip, and ying, in the yok ane yeir for to draw;
Fra I had preveit his pitht the first plesand moneth,   80
Than suld I cast me to keik in kirk, and in market,
And all the cintre about, kyngis court, and uther,
Quhair I ane galland micht get aganis the nixt yeir,
For to perfurneis furth the werk quhen failyeit the tother;
A forky fure, ay furthwart, and forsy in draucht,
Nother febill, nor fant, nor fulyeit in labour,
But als fresche of his forme as flouris in May;
For all the fruit suld I fang, thocht he the flour burgeoun.

I have ane wallidrag, ane worme, ane auld wobat carle,
A waistit wolroun, na worth bot wourdis to clatter;   90
Ane bumbart, ane dron bee, ane bag full of flewme,
Ane skabbit skarth, ane scorpioun, ane scutarde behind;
To see him scart his awin skyn grit scunner I think.
Quhen kissis me that carybald, than kyndillis all my sorow;
As birs of ane brym bair, his berd is als stif,
Bot soft and soupill as the silk is his sary lume;
He may weill to the syn assent, bot sakles is his deidis.
With goreis his tua grym ene ar gladderrit all about,
And gorgeit lyk twa gutaris that war with glar stoppit;
Bot quhen that glowrand gaist grippis me about,   100
Than think I hiddowus Mahowne hes me in armes;
Thair ma na sanyne me save fra that auld Sathane;
For, thocht I croce me all cleine, fra the croun doun,
He wil my corse all beclip, and clap me to his breist.
Quhen schaiffyne is that ald schalk with a scharp rasour,
He schowis one me his schevill mouth and schedis my lippis;
And with his hard hurcheone skyn sa heklis he my chekis,
That as a glemand gleyd glowis my chaftis;
I schrenk for the scharp stound, bot schout dar I nought,
For schore of that auld schrew, schame him betide!   110
The luf blenkis of that bogill, fra his blerde ene,
As Belzebub had on me blent, abasit my spreit;
And quhen the smy one me smyrkis with his smake smolet,
He fepillis like a farcy aver that flyrit one a gillot.
  Quhen that the sound of his saw sinkis in my eris,
Than ay renewis my noy, or he be neir cumand:
Quhen I heir nemmyt his name, than mak I nyne crocis,
To keip me fra the cummerans of that carll mangit,
That full of eldnyng is and anger and all evill thewis.
I dar nought luke to my luf for that lene gib,   120
He is sa full of jelusy and engyne fals;
Ever ymagynyng in mynd materis of evill,
Compasand and castand casis a thousand

How he sall tak me, with a trawe, at trist of ane othir:
I dar nought keik to the knaip that the cop fillis,
For eldnyng of that ald schrew that ever one evill thynkis;
For he is waistit and worne fra Venus werkis,
And may nought beit worth a bene in bed of my mystirs.
He trowis that young folk I yerne yeild, for he gane is,
Bot I may yuke all this yer, or his yerd help.   130
      Ay quhen that caribald carll wald clyme one my wambe,
Than am I dangerus and daine and dour of my will;
Yit leit I never that larbar my leggis ga betueene,
To fyle my flesche, na fumyll me, without a fee gret;
And thoght his pene purly me payis in bed,
His purse pays richely in recompense efter:
For, or he clym on my corse, that carybald forlane,
I have conditioun of a curche of kersp allther fynest,
A goun of engranyt claith, right gaily furrit,
A ring with a ryall stane, or other riche jowell,   140
Or rest of his rousty raid, thoght he wer rede wod:
For all the buddis of Johne Blunt, quhen he abone clymis,
Me think the baid deir aboucht, sa bawch ar his werkis;
And thus I sell him solace, thoght I it sour think:
Fra sic a syre, God yow saif, my sueit sisteris deir!
      Quhen that the semely had said her sentence to end,
Than all thai leuch apon loft with latis full mery,
And raucht the cop round about full of riche wynis,
And ralyeit lang, or thai wald rest, with ryatus speche.

The wedo to the tothir wlonk warpit ther wordis;   150
Now, fair sister, fallis yow but fenyeing to tell,
Sen man ferst with matrimony yow menskit in kirk,
How haif ye farne be your faith? confese us the treuth:
That band to blise, or to ban, quhilk yow best thinkis?
Or how ye like lif to leid in to leill spousage?
And syne my self ye exeme one the samyn wise,
And I sall say furth the south, dissymyland no word.

The plesand said, I protest, the treuth gif I schaw,
That of your toungis ye be traist. The tothir twa grantit;
With that sprang up hir spreit be a span hechar.   160
To speik, quoth scho, I sall nought spar; ther is no spy neir:
I sall a ragment reveil fra rute of my hert,
A roust that is sa rankild quhill risis my stomok;
Now sall the byle all out brist, that beild has so lang;
For it to beir one my brist wes berdin our hevy:
I sall the venome devoid with a vent large,
And me assuage of the swalme, that suellit wes gret.

My husband wes a hur maister, the hugeast in erd,
Tharfor I hait him with my hert, sa help me our Lord!
He is a young man ryght yaip, bot nought in youth flouris;   170
For he is fadit full far and feblit of strenth:
He wes as flurising fresche within this few yeris,
Bot he is falyeid full far and fulyeid in labour;
He has bene lychour so lang quhill lost is his natur,
His lume is waxit larbar, and lyis in to swonne:
Wes never sugeorne wer set na one that snaill tyrit,
For efter vii oulkis rest, it will nought rap anys;
He has bene waistit apone wemen, or he me wif chesit,
And in adultre, in my tyme, I haif him tane oft:
And yit he is als brankand with bonet one syde,   180
And blenkand to the brichtest that in the burgh duellis,
Alse curtly of his clething and kemmyng of his hair,
As he that is mare valyeand in Venus chalmer;
He semys to be sumthing worth, that syphyr in bour,
He lukis as he wald luffit be, thocht he is litill of valour;
He dois as dotit dog that damys on all bussis,
And liftis his leg apone loft, thoght he nought list pische;
He has a luke without lust and lif without curage;
He has a forme without force and fessoun but vertu,
And fair wordis but effect, all fruster of dedis;   190
He is for ladyis in luf a right lusty schadow,
Bot in to derne, at the deid, he salbe drup fundin;

He ralis, and makis repet with ryatus wordis,
Ay rusing him of his radis and rageing in chalmer;
Bot God wait quhat I think quhen he so thra spekis,
And how it settis him so syde to sege of sic materis.
Bot gif him self, of sum evin, mypht ane say amang thaim,
Bot he nought ane is, bot name of naturis possessoris.
    Scho that has ane auld man nought all is begylit;
He is at Venus werkis na war na he semys: 200
I wend I josit a gem, and I haif geit gottin;
He had the glemyng of gold, and wes bot glase fundin.
Thought men be ferse, wele I fynd, fra falye ther curage,
Thar is bot eldnyng or anger ther hertis within.
Ye speik of berdis one bewch: of blise may thai sing,
That, one Sanct Valentynis day, ar vacandis ilk yer;
Hed I that plesand prevelege to part quhen me likit,
To change, and ay to cheise agane, than, chastite, adew!
Than suld I haif a fresch feir to fang in myn armes:
To hald a freke, quhill he faynt, may foly be calit.   210
    Apone sic materis I mus, at mydnyght, full oft,
And murnys so in my mynd I murdris my selfin;
Than ly I walkand for wa, and walteris about,
Wariand oft my wekit kyn, that me away cast
To sic a craudoune but curage, that knyt my cler bewte,
And ther so mony kene knyghtis this kenrik within:
Than think I on a semelyar, the suth for to tell,
Na is our syre be sic sevin; with that I sych oft:
Than he ful tenderly dois turne to me his tume person,
And with a yoldin yerd dois yolk ne in armys,   220
And sais, 'My soverane sueit thing, quhy sleip ye no betir?
Me think ther haldis yow a hete, as ye sum harme alyt.'
Quoth I, 'My hony, hald abak, and handill me nought sair;
A hache is happinit hastely at my hert rut.'
With that I seme for to swoune, though I na swerf tak;
And thus beswik I that swane with my sueit wordis:
I cast on him a crabit E, quhen cleir day is cummyn,

98

And lettis it is a luf blenk, quhen he about glemys,
I turne it in a tender luke, that I in tene warit,
And him behaldis hamely with hertly smyling.   **230**
   I wald a tender peronall, that myght na put thole,
That hatit men with hard geir for hurting of flesch,
Had my gud man to hir gest; for I dar God suer,
Scho suld not stert for his straik a stray breid of erd.
And syne, I wald that ilk band, that ye so blist call,
Had bund him so to that bryght, quhill his bak werkit;
And I wer in a beid broght with berne that me likit,
I trow that bird of my blis suld a bourd want.

   Onone, quhen this amyable had endit hir speche,
Loudly lauchand the laif allowit hir mekle: **240**
Thir gay Wiffis maid game amang the grene leiffis;
Thai drank and did away dule under derne bewis;
Thai swapit of the sueit wyne, thai swanquhit of hewis,
Bot all the pertlyar in plane thai put out ther vocis.

   Than said the Weido, I wis ther is no way othir;
Now tydis me for to talk; my taill it is nixt:
God my spreit now inspir and my speche quykkin,
And send me sentence to say, substantious and noble;
Sa that my preching may pers your perverst hertis,
And mak yow mekar to men in maneris and conditiounis.   **250**
   I schaw yow, sisteris in schrift, I wes a schrew evir,
Bot I wes schene in my schrowd, and schew me innocent;
And thought I dour wes, and dane, dispitous, and bald,
I wes dissymblit suttelly in a sanctis liknes:
I semyt sober, and sueit, and sempill without fraud,
Bot I couth sexty dissaif that suttillar wer haldin.
   Unto my lesson ye lyth, and leir at me wit,
Gif you nought list be forleit with losingeris untrew:
Be constant in your governance, and counterfeit gud maneris,

Thought ye as tygris be terne, be tretable in luf, 260
And be as turtoris in your talk, thought ye haif talis brukill;
Be dragonis baith and dowis ay in double forme,
And quhen it nedis yow, onone, note baith ther strenthis;
Be amyable with humble face, as angellis apperand,
And with a terrebill tail be stangand as edderis;
Be of your luke like innocentis, thoght ye haif evill myndis;
Be courtly ay in clething and costly arrayit,
That hurtis yow nought worth a hen; yowr husband pays for all.
 Twa husbandis haif I had, thai held me baith deir,
Thought I dispytit thaim agane, thai spyit it na thing: 270
Ane wes ane hair hogeart, that hostit out flewme;
I hatit him like a hund, thought I it hid preve:
With kissing and with clapping I gert the carll fone;
Weil couth I keyth his cruke bak, and kemm his cowit noddill,
And with a bukky in my cheik bo on him behind,
And with a bek gang about and bler his ald E,
And with a kynd contynance kys his crynd chekis;
In to my mynd makand mokis at that mad fader,
Trowand me with trew lufe to treit him so fair.
This cought I do without dule and na dises tak,
Bot ay be mery in my mynd and myrth full of cher. 280
 I had a lufsummar leid my lust for to slokyn,
That couth be secrete and sure and ay saif my honour,
And sew bot at certayne tymes and in sicir placis;
Ay when the ald did me anger, with akword wordis,
Apon the galland for to goif it gladit me agane.
I had sic wit that for wo weipit I litill,
Bot leit the sueit ay the sour to gud sesone bring.
Quhen that the chuf wald me chid, with girnand chaftis,
I wald him chuk, cheik and chyn, and cheris him so mekill, 290
That his cheif chymys he had chevist to my sone,
Suppose the churll wes gane chaist, or the child wes gottin:
As wis woman ay I wrought and not as wod fule,
For mar with wylis I wan na wichtnes of handis.

Syne maryit I a marchand, myghti of gudis:
He was a man of myd eld and of mene statur;
Bot we na fallowis wer in frendschip or blud,
In fredome, na furth bering, na fairnes of persoune,
Quhilk ay the fule did foryhet, for febilnes of knawlege,
Bot I sa oft thoght him on, quhill angrit his hert,   300
And quhilum I put furth my voce and Pedder him callit:
I wald ryght tuichandly talk be I wes tuyse maryit,
For endit wes my innocence with my ald husband:
I wes apperand to be pert within perfit eild;
Sa sais the curat of our kirk, that knew me full ying:
He is our famous to be fals, that fair worthy prelot;
I salbe laith to lat him le, quhill I may luke furth.
I gert the buthman obey, ther wes no bute ellis;
He maid me ryght hie reverens, fra he my rycht knew:
For, thocht I say it my self, the severance wes mekle   310
Betuix his bastard blude and my birth noble.
That page wes never of sic price for to presome anys
Unto my persone to be peir, had pete nought grantit.
Bot mercy in to womanheid is a mekle vertu,
For never bot in a gentill hert is generit ony ruth.
I held ay grene in to his mynd that I of grace tuk him,
And for he couth ken him self I curtasly him lerit:
He durst not sit anys my summondis, for, or the secund charge,
He wes ay redy for to ryn, so rad he wes for blame.
Bot ay my will wes the war of womanly natur;   320
The mair he loutit for my luf, the les of him I rakit;
And eik, this is a ferly thing, or I him faith gaif,
I had sic favour to that freke, and feid syne for ever.
    Quhen I the cure had all clene and him ourcummyn haill,
I crew abone that craudone, as cok that wer victour;
Quhen I him saw subject and sett at myn bydding,
Than I him lichtlyit as a lowne and lathit his maneris.
Than woxe I sa unmerciable to martir him I thought,
For as a best I broddit him to all boyis laubour:

I wald haif ridden him to Rome with raip in his heid, 330
Wer not ruffill of my renoune and rumour of pepill.
And yit hatrent I hid within my hert all;
Bot quhilis it hepit so huge, quhill it behud out:
Yit tuk I nevir the wosp clene out of my wyde throte,
Quhill I oucht wantit of my will or quhat I wald desir.
Bot quhen I severit had that syre of substance in erd,
And gottin his biggingis to my barne, and hie burrow landis,
Than with a stew stert out the stoppell of my hals,
That he all stunyst throu the stound, as of a stele wappin.
Than wald I, efter lang, first sa fane haif bene wrokin, 340
That I to flyte wes als fers as a fell dragoun.
I had for flattering of that fule fenyeit so lang,
Mi evidentis of heritagis or thai wer all selit,
My breist, that wes gret beild, bowdyn wes sa huge,
That neir my baret out brist or the band makin.
Bot quhen my billis and my bauchles wes all braid selit,
I wald na langar beir on bridill, bot braid up my heid;
Thar myght na molet mak me moy, na hald my mouth in:
I gert the renyeis rak and rif into sondir;
I maid that wif carll to werk all womenis werkis, 350
And laid all manly materis and mensk in this eird.
Than said I to my cumaris in counsall about,
'Se how I cabeld yone cout with a kene brydill!
The cappill, that the crelis kest in the caf mydding,
Sa curtasly the cart drawis, and kennis na plungeing,
He is nought skeich, na yit sker, na scippis nought one syd':
And thus the scorne and the scaith scapit he nothir.

    He was no glaidsum gest for a gay lady,
Tharfor I gat him a game that ganyt him bettir;
He wes a gret goldit man and of gudis riche; 360
I leit him be my lumbart to lous me all misteris,
And he was fane for to fang fra me that fair office,
And thoght my favoris to fynd through his feill giftis.
He grathit me in a gay silk and gudly arrayis,

102

In gownis of engranyt claith and gret goldin chenyeis,
In ringis ryally set with riche ruby stonis,
Quhill hely raise my renoune amang the rude peple.
Bot I full craftely did keip thai courtly wedis,
Quhill eftir dede of that drupe, that dotht nought in chalmir:
Thought he of all my clathis maid cost and expense,   370
Ane othir sall the worschip haif, that weildis me eftir;
And thoght I likit him bot litill, yit for luf of otheris,
I wald me prunya plesandly in precius wedis,
That luffaris myght apone me luke and ying lusty gallandis,
That I held more in daynte and derer be ful mekill
Ne him that dressit me so dink: full dotit wes his heyd.
Quhen he wes heryit out of hand to hie up my honoris,
And payntit me as pako, proudest of fedderis,
I him miskennyt, be Crist, and cukkald him maid;
I him forleit as a lad and lathlyit him mekle: 380
I thoght my self a papingay and him a plukit herle;
All thus enforsit he his fa and fortifyit in strenth,
And maid a stalwart staff to strik him selfe doune.

   Bot of ane bowrd in to bed I sall yow breif yit:
Quhen he ane hail year was hanyt, and him behuffit rage,
And I wes laith to be loppin with sic a lob avoir,
Alse lang as he wes on loft, I lukit on him never,
Na leit never enter in my thoght that he my thing persit,
Bot ay in mynd ane other man ymagynit that I haid
Or ellis had I never mery bene at that myrthles raid.   390
Quhen he had warit all one me his welth and his substance,
Me thoght his wit wes all went away with the laif;
And so I did him despise, I spittit quhen I saw
That super spendit evill spreit, spulyeit of all vertu.
For, weill ye wait, wiffis, that he that wantis riches
And valyeandnes in Venus play, is ful vile haldin:
Full fruster is his fresch array and fairnes of persoune,
All is bot frutlese his effeir and falyeis at the up with.

   I buskit up my barnis like baronis sonnis,

And maid bot fulis of the fry of his first wif.   400
I banyst fra my boundis his brethir ilkane;
His frendis as my fais I held at feid evir;
Be this, ye belief may, I luffit nought him self,
For never I likit a leid that langit till his blude:
And yit thir wisemen, thai wait that all wiffis evill
Ar kend with ther conditionis and knawin with the samin.

  Deid is now that dyvour and dollin in erd:
With him deit all my dule and my drery thoghtis;
Now done is my dolly nyght, my day is upsprungin,
Adew dolour, adew! my daynte now begynis: 410
Now am I a wedow, I wise and weill am at ese;
I weip as I were woful, but wel is me for ever;
I busk as I wer bailfull, bot blith is my hert:
My mouth it makis murnyng, and my mynd lauchis;
My clokis thai ar caerfull in colour of sabill,
Bot courtly and ryght curyus my corse is ther undir:
I drup with a ded luke in my dule habit,
As with manis daill [I] had done for dayis of my lif.

  Quhen that I go to the kirk, cled in cair weid,
As foxe in a lambis fleise fenye I my cheir;   420
Than lay I furght my bright buke one breid one my kne,
With mony lusty letter ellummynit with gold;
And drawis my clok forthwart our my face quhit,
That I may spy, unaspyit, a space me beside:
Full oft I blenk by my buke, and blynis of devotioun,
To se quhat berne is best brand or bredest in schulderis,
Or forgeit is maist forcely to furnyse a bancat
In Venus chalmer, valyeandly, withoutin vane ruse:
And, as the new mone all pale, oppressit with change,
Kythis quhilis her cleir face through cluddis of sable,   430
So keik I through my clokis, and castis kynd lukis
To knychtis, and to cleirkis, and cortly personis.

  Quhen frendis of my husbandis behaldis me one fer,
I haif a watter spunge for wa, within my wyde clokis,

Than wring I it full wylely and wetis my chekis,
With that watteris myn ene and welteris doune teris.
Than say thai all, that sittis about, 'Se ye nought, allace!
Yone lustlese led so lelely scho luffit hir husband:
Yone is a pete to enprent in a princis hert,
That sic a perle of plesance suld yone pane dre!'   440
I sane me as I war ane sanct, and semys ane angell;
At langage of lichory I leit as I war crabit:
I sich, without sair hert or seiknes in body;
According to my sable weid I mon haif sad maneris,
Or thai will se all the suth; for certis, we wemen
We set us all fra the syght to syle men of treuth:
We dule for na evill deid, sa it be derne haldin.

    Wise wemen has wayis and wonderfull gydingis
With gret engyne to bejaip ther jolyus husbandis;
And quyetly, with sic craft, convoyis our materis   450
That, under Crist, no creatur kennis of our doingis.
Bot folk a cury may miscuke, that knawledge wantis,
And has na colouris for to cover thair awne kindly fautis;
As dois thir damysellis, for derne dotit lufe,
That dogonis haldis in dainte and delis with thaim so lang,
Quhill all the cuntre knaw ther kyndnes and faith:
Faith has a fair name, bot falsheid faris bettir:
Fy one hir that can nought feyne her fame for to saif!
Yit am I wise in sic werk and wes all my tyme;
Thoght I want wit in warldlynes, I wylis haif in luf,   460
As ony happy woman has that is of hie blude:
Hutit be the halok las a hunder yeir of eild!

    I have ane secrete servand, rycht sobir of his toung,
That me supportis of sic nedis, quhen I a syne mak:
Thoght he be sympill to the sicht, he has a tong sickir;
Full mony semelyar sege wer service dois mak:
Thought I haif cair, under cloke, the cleir day quhill nygt
Yit haif I solace, under serk, quhill the sone ryse.

    Yit am I haldin a haly wif our all the haill schyre,

I am sa peteouse to the pur, quhen ther is personis mony.   470
In passing of pilgrymage I pride me full mekle,
Mair for the prese of peple na ony perdoun wynyng.
   Bot yit me think the best bourd, quhen baronis and knychtis,
And othir bachilleris, blith blumyng in youth,
And all my luffaris lele, my lugeing persewis,
And fyllis me wyne wantonly with weilfair and joy:
Sum rownis; and sum ralyeis; and sum redis ballatis;
Sum raiffis furght rudly with riatus speche;
Sum plenis, and sum prayis; sum prasis mi bewte,
Sum kissis me; sum clappis me; sum kyndnes me proferis;   480
Sum kerffis to me curtasli; sum me the cop giffis;
Sum stalwardly steppis ben, with a stout curage,
And a stif standand thing staiffis in my neiff;
And mony blenkis ben our, that but full for sittis,
That mai, for the thik thrang, nought thrif as thai wald.
Bot, with my fair calling, I comfort thaim all:
For he that sittis me nixt, I nip on his finger;
I serf him on the tothir syde on the samin fasson;
And he that behind me sittis, I hard on him lene;
And him befor, with my fut fast on his I stramp;   490
And to the bernis far but sueit blenkis I cast:
To every man in speciall speke I sum wordis
So wisly and so womanly, quhill warmys ther hertis.
   Thar is no liffand leid so law of degre
That sall me luf unluffit, I am so loik hertit;
And gif his lust so be lent into my lyre quhit,
That he be lost or with me lig, his lif sall nocht danger.
I am so mercifull in mynd, and menys all wichtis,
My sely saull salbe saif, quhen sa bot all jugis.
Ladyis leir thir lessonis and be no lassis fundin: 500
This is the legeand of my lif, thought Latyne it be nane.

   Quhen endit had her ornat speche, this eloquent wedow,
Lowd thai lewch all the laif, and loffit hir mekle;

And said thai suld exampill tak of her soverane teching,
And wirk efter hir wordis, that woman wes so prudent.
Than culit thai thair mouthis with confortable drinkis;
And carpit full cummerlik with cop going round.

   Thus draif thai our that deir nyght with danceis full noble,
Quhill that the day did up daw, and dew donkit flouris;
The morow myld wes and meik, the mavis did sing,   510
And all remuffit the myst, and the meid smellit;
Silver schouris doune schuke as the schene cristall,
And berdis schoutit in schaw with thair schill notis;
The goldin glitterand gleme so gladit ther hertis,
Thai maid a glorius gle amang the grene bewis.
The soft sowch of the swyr and soune of the stremys,
The sueit savour of the sward and singing of foulis,
Myght confort ony creatur of the kyn of Adam,
And kindill agane his curage, thocht it wer cald sloknyt.
   Than rais thir ryall roisis, in ther riche wedis,   520
And rakit hame to ther rest through the rise blumys;
And I all prevely past to a plesand arber,
And with my pen did report thair pastance most mery.

   Ye auditoris most honorable, that eris has gevin
Oneto this uncouth aventur, quhilk airly me happinnit;
Of thir thre wantoun wiffis, that I haif writtin heir,
Quhilk wald ye waill to your wif, gif ye suld wed one?

(Mackenzie, Poems of Dunbar)

His panefull purs

Sanct Salvatour, send silver sorrow!
It grevis me both evin and morrow,
Chasing fra me all cheritie.

It makis me all blythness to borrow,
My panefull purs so priclis me.

Quhen I wald blythlie ballattis breif,
Langour thairto givis no leif.
War nocht gud howp my hart uphie
My verry corpis for cair wald cleif.
My panefull purs so prikillis me.   10

Quhen I sett me to sing or dance,
Or go to plesand pastance,
Than pansing of penuritie
Revis that fra my remembrance,
My panefull purs so prikillis me.

Quhen men that hes pursis in tone
Pasis to drynk or to disjone,
Than mon I keip ane gravetie
And say that I will fast quhill none,
My panefull purs so priclis me.   20

My purs is maid of sic ane skyn
Thair will na cors byd it within:
Fra it as fra the Feynd thay fle.
Quha evir tyne, quha evir win,
My panefull purs so prikillis me.

Had I ane man of ony natioun
Culd mak on it ane conjuratioun
To gar silver ay in it be,
The Devill suld haif no dominatioun
With pyne to gar it prickill me.   30

I haif inquyrit in mony a place
For help and confort in this cace,

And all men sayis, My Lord, that ye
Can best remeid for this malice
That with sic panis prickillis me.

(Mackenzie, *Poems of Dunbar*)

Remonstrance to the King

Schir, ye have mony servitouris
And officiaris of dyvers curis;
Kirkmen, courtmen, and craftismen fyne;
Doctouris in jure, and medicyne;
Divinouris, rethoris, and philosophouris,
Astrologis, artistis, and oratouris;
Men of armes, and vailyeand knychtis,
And mony uther gudlie wichtis;
Musicianis, menstralis, and mirrie singaris:
Chevalouris, cawandaris, and flingaris;   10
Cunyouris, carvoris, and carpentaris,
Beildaris of barkis and ballingaris;
Masounis lyand upon the land,
And schipwrichtis hewand upone the strand;
Glasing wrichtis, goldsmythis, and lapidaris,
Pryntouris, payntouris, and potingaris;
And all thair craft cunning,
And all at anis lawboring;
Quhilk pleisand ar and honorable,
And to your hienes profitable,   20
And richt convenient for to be
With your hie regale majestie;
Deserving of your grace most ding
Bayth thank, rewarde, and cherissing.
  And thocht that I, amang the laif,
Unworthy be ane place to have,

Or in thair nummer to be tald,
Als lang in mynd my wark sall hald,
Als haill in everie circumstance,
In forme, in mater, and substance,   30
But wering, or consumptioun,
Roust, canker, or corruptioun,
As ony of thair werkis all,
Suppois that my rewarde be small.
　Bot ye sa gracious ar and meik,
That on your hienes followis eik
Ane uthir sort, more miserabill,
Thocht thai be nocht sa profitable:
Fenyeouris, fleichouris, and flatteraris;
Cryaris, craikaris, and clatteraris;   40
Soukaris, groukaris, gledaris, gunnaris;
Monsouris of France, gud clarat-cunnaris;
Innopportoun askaris of Yrland kynd;
And meit revaris, lyk out of mynd;
Scaffaris, and scamleris in the nuke,
And hall huntaris of draik and duik;
Thrimlaris and thristaris, as thay war woid,
Kokenis, and kennis na man of gude;
Schulderaris, and schowaris, that hes no schame,
And to no cunning that can clame;   50
And can non uthir craft nor curis
Bot to mak thrang, Schir, in your duris,
And rusche in quhair thay counsale heir,
And will at na man nurtir leyr:
In quintiscence, eik, ingynouris joly,
That far can multiplie in folie;
Fantastik fulis, bayth fals and gredy,
Off toung untrew, and hand evill deidie:
Few dar, of all this last additioun,
Cum in tolbuyth without remissioun.   60
　And thocht this nobill cunning sort,

Quhom of befoir I did report,
Rewardit be, it war bot ressoun,
Thairat suld no man mak enchessoun.
Bot quhen the uther fulis nyce,
That feistit at Cokelbeis gryce,
Ar all rewardit, and nocht I,
Than on this fals world I cry, Fy!
My hart neir bristis than for teyne,
Quhilk may nocht suffer nor sustane   70
So grit abusioun for to se,
Daylie in court befoir myn E!

   And yit more panence wald I have,
Had I rewarde amang the laif,
It wald me sumthing satisfie,
And les of my malancolie,
And gar me mony falt ouerse,
That now is brayd befoir myn E:
My mind so fer is set to flyt,
That of nocht ellis I can endyt;   80
For owther man my hart to breik,
Or with my pen I man me wreik;
And sen the tane most nedis be,
In to malancolie to de,
Or lat the vennim ische all out,
Be war, anone, for it will spout,
Gif that the tryackill cum nocht tyt
To swage the swalme of my dispyt!

(Mackenzie, *Poems of Dunbar*)

Of a Dance in the Quenis Chalmer

Schir Jhon Sinclair begowthe to dance,
For he was new cum owt of France;

For ony thing that he do mycht,
The ane futt yeid ay onrycht,
    And to the tother wald not gree.
Quod ane, 'Tak up the Quenis knycht':
    A mirrear dance mycht na man see.

Than cam in Maistir Robert Scha:
He leuket as he culd lern tham a;
Bot ay his ane futt did waver,   10
He stackeret lyk ane strummall aver,
    That hopschackellt war aboin the kne:
To seik fra Sterling to Stranaver,
    A mirrear daunce mycht na man see.

Than cam in the Maister Almaser,
Ane hommiltye jommeltye juffler,
Lyk a stirk stackarand in the ry;
His hippis gaff mony hoddous cry.
    John Bute the Fule said, 'Waes me!
He is bedirtin,—Fye! fy!'   20
    A mirrear dance mycht na man se.

Than cam in Dunbar the Mackar;
On all the flure thair was nane frackar,
And thair he dancet the dirrye dantoun;
He hoppet lyk a pillie wanton,
    For luff of Musgraeffe, men tellis me;
He trippet, quhill he tint his panton:
    A mirrear dance mycht na man se.

Than cam in Maesteres Musgraeffe;
Scho mycht heff lernit all the laeffe;   30
Quhen I schau hir sa trimlye dance,
Hir guid convoy and contenance,
    Than, for hir saek, I wissitt to be

The grytast erle or duk in France:
    A mirrear dance mycht na man see.

Than cam in Dame Dounteboir;
God waett gif that schou louket sowr!
Schou maid sic morgeownis with hir hippis;
For lachtter nain mycht hald thair lippis;
    Quhen schou was danceand bisselye,   40
Ane blast of wind son fra hir slippis:
    A mirrear dance mycht na man see.

Quhen thair was cum in fyve or sax,
The Quenis Dog begowthe to rax,
And of his band he maid a bred,
And to the danceing soin he him med;
    Quhou mastevlyk about yeid he!
He stinckett lyk a tyk, sum saed:
    A mirrear dance mycht na man se.

(Mackenzie, *Poems of Dunbar*)

The Petition of the Gray Horse, Auld Dunbar

Now lufferis cummis with larges lowd,
Quhy sould not palfrayis thane be prowd,
Quhen gillettis wil be schomd and schroud,
That ridden ar baith with lord and lawd?
   Schir, lat it nevir in toun be tald,
   That I suld be ane Youllis yald!

Quhen I was young and into ply,
And wald cast gammaldis to the sky,
I had beine bocht in realmes by,

Had I consentit to be sauld.
 Schir, lett it nevir in toun be tauld,
 That I suld be ane Youllis yald!

With gentill hors quehn I wald knyp,
Thane is thair laid on me ane quhip,
To colleveris than man I skip,
That scabbit ar, hes cruik and cald,
 Schir, lett it nevir in toun be tald,
 That I suld be ane Youllis yald!

Thocht in the stall I be not clappit,
As cursouris that in silk beine trappit,
With ane new hous I wald be hapit,
Aganis this Crysthinmes for the cald.
 Schir, lett it nevir in toun be tald,
 That I suld be ane Yuillis yald!

Suppois I war ane ald yaid aver,
Schott furth our clewch to squische the clever,
And hed the strenthis off all Strenever,
I wald at Youll be housit and stald,
 Schir, lat it never in toune be tald,
 That I suld be ane Yuillis yald!

I am ane auld hors, as ye knaw,
That ever in duill dois drug and draw;
Great court hors puttis me fra the staw,
To fang the fog be firthe and fald.
 Schir, lat it never in toune be tald,
 That I suld be ane Yuillis yald!

I heff run lang furth in the feild
On pastouris that ar plane and peld;
I mycht be now tein in for eild,

My bekis ar spruning he and bald.　　　　　**40**
　　Schir, lat it never in toun be tald,
　　That I suld be ane Yuillis yald!

My maine is turned in to quhyt,
And thair off ye heff all the wyt!
Quhen uthair hors hed brane to byt
I gat bot gris, grype giff I wald.
　　Schir, lat it never in towne be tald,
　　That I suld be ane Yuillis yald!

I was never dautit in to stabell,
My lyff hes bein so miserabell,　　　　　**50**
My hyd to offer I am abell,
For evill schoud strae that I reiv wald.
　　Schir, lat it never in towne be tald,
　　That I suld be ane Yuillis yald!

And yett, suppois my thrift be thyne,
Gif that I die your aucht within,
Lat nevir the soutteris have my skin,
With uglie gumes to be gnawin.
　　Schir, lat it nevir in toun be tald,
　　That I suld be ane Yuillis yald!　　　　　**60**

The court hes done my curage cuill,
And maid me ane forriddin muill;
Yett, to weir trapperis at the Yuill,
I wald be spurrit at everie spald.
　　Schir, lat it nevir in toun be tald,
　　That I suld be ane Yuillis yald!

Efter our wrettingis, thesaurer,
Tak in this gray hors, Auld Dumbar,
Quhilk in my aucht with service trew
In lyart changeit is in hew, 70
Gar hows him now aganis this Yuill,
And busk him lyk ane bischopis muill,
For with my hand I have indost
To pay quhatevir his trappouris cost.

(Mackenzie, *Poems of Dunbar*)

To a Ladye

Sweit rois of vertew and of gentilnes,
Delytsum lyllie of everie lustynes,
 Richest in bontie and in bewtie cleir,
 And everie vertew that is [held most] deir,
Except onlie that ye ar mercyles.

In to your garthe this day I did persew,
Thair saw I flowris that fresche wer of hew;
 Baith quhyte and reid moist lusty wer to seyne,
 And halsum herbis upone stalkis grene;
Yit leif nor flour fynd could I nane of rew. 10

I dout that Merche, with his caild blastis keyne,
Hes slane this gentill herbe that I of mene,
 Quhois petewous deithe dois to my hart sic pane

That I wald mak to plant his rute agane.
So confortand his levis unto me bene.

(Mackenzie, *Poems of Dunbar*)

On his heid-ake

My heid did yak yester nicht,
This day to mak that I na micht,
   So sair the magryme dois me menyie,
   Perseing my brow as ony ganyie,
That scant I luik may on the licht.

And now, schir, laitlie, eftir mes,
To dyt thocht I begowthe to dres,
   The sentence lay full evill till find,
   Unsleipit in my heid behind,
Dulkit in dulnes and distres.   10

Full oft at morrow I upryse,
Quhen that my curage sleipeing lyis,
   For mirth, for menstrallie and play,
   For din nor danceing nor deray,
It will nocht walkin me no wise.

(Mackenzie, *Poems of Dunbar*)

Meditatioun in Wyntir

In to thir dirk and drublie dayis,
Quhone sabill all the hevin arrayis

With mystie vapouris, cluddis, and skyis,
Nature all curage me denyis
Off sangis, ballattis, and of playis.

Quhone that the nycht dois lenthin houris,
With wind, with haill, and havy schouris,
    My dule spreit dois lurk for schoir,
    My hairt for languor dois forloir
For laik of symmer with his flouris.   10

I walk, I turne, sleip may I nocht,
I vexit am with havie thocht;
    This warld all ouir I cast about,
    And ay the mair I am in dout,
The mair that I remeid have socht.

I am assayit on everie syde:
Dispair sayis ay, 'In tyme provyde
    And get sum thing quhairon to leif,
    Or with grit trouble and mischeif
Thow sall in to this court abyd.'   20

Than Patience sayis, 'Be not agast:
Hald Hoip and Treuthe within the fast,
    And lat Fortoun wirk furthe hir rage,
    Quhome that no rasoun may assuage,
Quhill that hir glas be run and past.'

And Prudence in my eir sayis ay,
'Quhy wald thow hald that will away?
    Or craif that thow may have no space,
    Thow tending to ane uther place,
A journay going everie day?'   30

And than sayis Age, 'My freind, cum neir,
And be not strange, I the requeir:
  Cum, brodir, by the hand me tak,
  Remember thow hes compt to mak
Off all thi tyme thow spendit heir.'

Syne Deid castis upe his yettis wyd,
Saying, 'Thir oppin sall the abyd;
  Albeid that thow wer never sa stout,
  Undir this lyntall sall thow lowt:
Thair is nane uther way besyde.'   40

For feir of this all day I drowp;
No gold in kist, nor wyne in cowp,
  No ladeis bewtie, nor luiffis blys,
  May lat me to remember this,
How glaid that ever I dyne or sowp.

Yit, quhone the nycht begynnis to schort,
It dois my spreit sum pairt confort,
  Off thocht oppressit with the schowris.
  Cum, lustie symmer! with thi flowris,
That I may leif in sum disport.   50

(Mackenzie, *Poems of Dunbar*)

Lament for the Makaris
'Quhen He Wes Sek'

I that in heill wes and gladnes,
Am trublit now with gret seiknes,
And feblit with infermite;
  Timor mortis conturbat me.

Our plesance heir is all vane glory,
This fals warld is bot transitory,
The flesche is brukle, the Fend is sle;
   Timor mortis conturbat me.

The stait of man dois change and vary,
Now sound, now seik, now blith, now sary,   10
Now dansand mery, now like to dee;
   Timor mortis conturbat me.

No stait in erd heir standis sickir;
As with the wynd wavis the wickir,
Wavis this warldis vanite;
   Timor mortis conturbat me.

On to the ded gois all Estatis,
Princis, Prelotis, and Potestatis,
Baith riche and pur of al degre;
   Timor mortis conturbat me.   20

He takis the knychtis in to feild,
Anarmit under helme and scheild;
Victour he is at all mellie;
   Timor mortis conturbat me.

That strang unmercifull tyrand
Takis, on the moderis breist sowkand,
The bab full of benignite;
   Timor mortis conturbat me.

He takis the campion in the stour,
The capitane closit in the tour,   30
The lady in bour full of bewte;
   Timor mortis conturbat me.

He sparis no lord for his piscence;
Na clerk for his intelligence;
His awfull strak may no man fle;
    Timor mortis conturbat me.

Art, magicianis, and astrologgis,
Rethoris, logicianis, and theologgis,
Thame helpis no conclusionis sle;
    Timor mortis conturbat me.   40

In medicyne the most practicianis,
Lechis, surrigianis, and phisicianis,
Thame self fra ded may not supple;
    Timor mortis conturbat me.

I se that makaris amang the laif
Playis heir ther pageant, syne gois to graif;
Sparit is nocht ther faculte;
    Timor mortis conturbat me.

He hes done petuously devour,
The noble Chaucer, of makaris flour,   50
The Monk of Bery, and Gower, all thre;
    Timor mortis conturbat me.

The gude Syr Hew of Eglintoun,
And eik Heryot, and Wyntoun,
He hes tane out of this cuntre;
    Timor mortis conturbat me.

That scorpion fell hes done infek
Maister Johne Clerk, and James Afflek,
Fra balat making and tragidie;
    Timor mortis conturbat mc.   60

Holland and Barbour he hes berevit;
Allace! that he nocht with us levit
Schir Mungo Lokert of the Le;
   Timor mortis conturbat me.

Clerk of Tranent eik he hes tane,
That maid the Anteris of Gawane;
Schir Gilbert Hay endit hes he;
   Timor mortis conturbat me.

He hes Blind Hary and Sandy Traill
Slaine with his schour of mortall haill,   70
Quhilk Patrik Johnestoun mycht nocht fle;
   Timor mortis conturbat me.

He hes reft Merseir his endite,
That did in luf so lifly write,
So schort, so quyk, of sentence hie;
   Timor mortis conturbat me.

He hes tane Roull of Aberdene,
And gentill Roull of Corstorphin;
Two bettir fallowis did no man se;
   Timor mortis conturbat me.   80

In Dumfermelyne he hes done roune
With Maister Robert Henrisoun;
Schir Johne the Ros enbrast hes he;
   Timor mortis conturbat me.

And he hes now tane, last of aw,
Gud gentill Stobo and Quintyne Schaw,
Of quham all wichtis hes pete:
   Timor mortis conturbat me.

Gud Maister Walter Kennedy
In poynt of dede lyis veraly,   90
Gret reuth it wer that so suld be;
   Timor mortis conturbat me.

Sen he hes all my brether tane,
He will nocht lat me lif alane,
On forse I man his nyxt pray be;
   Timor mortis conturbat me.

Sen for the deid remeid is none,
Best is that we for dede dispone,
Eftir our deid that lif may we;
   Timor mortis conturbat me.   100

(Mackenzie, Poems of Dunbar)

To the Merchantis of Edinburgh

Quhy will ye, merchantis of renoun,
Lat Edinburgh, your nobill toun,
For laik of reformatioun
The commone proffeitt tyine and fame?
   Think ye not schame,
That onie uther regioun
Sall with dishonour hurt your name!

May nane pas throw your principall gaittis
For stink of haddockis and of scattis,
For cryis of carlingis and debaittis,   10
For fensum flyttingis of defame:
   Think ye not schame,
Befoir strangeris of all estaittis
That sic dishonour hurt your name!

Your stinkand Styll, that standis dirk,
Haldis the lycht fra your parroche kirk;
Your foirstairis makis your housis mirk,
Lvk na cuntray bot heir at hame:
    Think ye not schame,
Sa litill polesie to wirk   20
In hurt and sklander of your name!

At your hie Croce, quhar gold and silk
Sould be, thair is bot crudis and milk;
And at your Trone bot cokill and wilk,
Pansches, pudingis of Jok and Jame:
    Think ye not schame,
Sen as the world sayis that ilk
In hurt and sclander of your name!

Your commone menstrallis hes no tone
Bot 'Now the day dawis,' and 'Into Joun';   30
Cunningar men man serve Sanct Cloun,
And nevir to uther craftis clame:
    Think ye not schame,
To hald sic mowaris on the moyne,
In hurt and sclander of your name!

Tailyouris, soutteris, and craftis vyll,
The fairest of your streitis dois fyll;
And merchandis at the Stinkand Styll
Ar hamperit in ane hony came:
    Think ye not schame,   40
That ye have nether witt nor wyll
To win yourselff ane bettir name!

Your burgh of beggeris is ane nest,
To schout thai swentyouris will not rest;
All honest folk they do molest,

Sa piteuslie thai cry and rame:
    Think ye not schame,
That for the poore hes nothing drest,
In hurt and sclander of your name!

Your proffeit daylie dois incres,   50
Your godlie workis les and les;
Through streittis nane may mak progres
For cry of cruikit, blind, and lame:
    Think ye not schame,
That ye sic substance dois posses,
And will nocht win ane bettir name!

Sen for the Court and the Sessioun,
The great repair of this regioun
Is in your burgh, thairfoir be boun
To mend all faultis that ar to blame,   60
    And eschew schame;
Gif thai pas to ane uther toun
Ye will decay, and your great name!

Thairfoir strangeris and leigis treit,
Tak not ouer meikle for thair meit,
And gar your merchandis be discreit,
That na extortiounes be, proclame
    All fraud and schame:
Keip ordour, and poore nighbouris beit,
That ye may gett ane bettir name!   70

Singular proffeit so dois yow blind,
The common proffeit gois behind:
I pray that Lord remeid to fynd,
That deit into Jerusalem,

And gar yow schame!
That sum tyme ressoun may yow bind,
For to [   ] yow guid name.

(Mackenzie, *Poems of Dunbar*)

On the Resurrection of Christ

Done is a battell on the dragon blak,
Our campioun Chryst confountet hes his force;
The yettis of hell ar brokin with a crak,
The signe triumphall rasit is of the croce,
The divillis trymmillis with hiddous voce,
The saulis ar borrowit and to the blis can go,
Chryst with his blud our ransonis dois indoce:
Surrexit Dominus de sepulchro.

Dungin is the deidly dragon Lucifer,
The crewall serpent with the mortall stang;   10
The auld kene tegir with his teith on char,
Quhilk in a wait hes lyne for us so lang,
Thinking to grip us in his clows strang;
The mercifull Lord wald nocht that it wer so,
He maid him for to felye of that fang:
Surrexit Dominus de sepulchro.

He for our saik that sufferit to be slane,
And lyk a lamb in sacrifice wes dicht,
Is lyk a lyone rissin up agane,
And as gyane raxit him on hicht;   20
Sprungin is Aurora radius and bricht,
On loft is gone the glorius Appollo,
The blisfull day depairtit fro the nycht:
Surrexit Dominus de sepulchro.

The grit victour agane is rissin on hicht,
That for our querrell to the deth wes woundit;
The sone that wox all paill now schynis bricht,
And dirknes clerit, our fayth is now refoundit;
The knell of mercy fra the hevin is soundit,
The Cristin ar deliverit of thair wo,   30
The Jowis and thair errour ar confoundit:
Surrexit Dominus de sepulchro.

The fo is chasit, the battell is done ceis,
The presone brokin, the jevellouris fleit and flemit;
The weir is gon, confermit is the peis,
The fetteris lowsit and the dungeoun temit,
The ransoun maid, the presoneris redemit;
The feild is win, ourcumin is the fo,
Dispulit of the tresur that he yemit:
Surrexit Dominus de sepulchro.   40

(Mackenzie, *Poems of Dunbar*)

GAWIN DOUGLAS

The Palice of Honour, II.*xvii*

Sa greit ane preis of pepill drew us neir
The hundredth part thair names ar not heir,
Yit saw I thair of Brutus Albyon,
Geffray Chauceir, as *a per se* sans peir
In his vulgare, and morall Johne Goweir.
Lydgait the monk raid musing him allone.
Of this natioun I knew also anone
Greit Kennedie, and Dunbaɪ yit undeid,
And Quintine with ane huttock on his heid.

From *The Eneados* (*Aeneid*)

First Proloug, 105–26

First I protest, beawschiris, be your leif,
Beis weill advisit my werk or ye repreif;
Considdir it warlie, reid oftair than anis;
Weill at ane blenk slee poetry nocht tane is
And yit, forsuith, I set my besy pane
As that I culd, to mak it braid and plane,
Kepand na sudroun, bot our awin langage,
And speikis as I lerit quhen I was page . . .
Nor yit sa clene all sudroun I refuse,
Bot sum word I pronunce as nychtbour doise;   10
Lyk as in Latyne bene Grew termes sum,

So me behuvit quhilum, or than be dum,
Sum bastard Latyne, Frensch, or Inglis oiss,
Quhar scant war Scottis I had na uther choiss.
Nocht for our toung is in the selfin scant
Bot for that I the foutht of langage want,
Quhair as the colour of his propirte
To keip the sentence thairto constrenit me,
Or than to mak my sang, schort sum tyme,
Mair compendious, or to liklie my ryme.   20
Therfor, guid freindis, for ane jymp or a bourd,
I pray you note me nocht at every wourd.

(Goodsir Smith, Saltire Classics edition)

The Prologue to Book VII

As bryght Phebus, scheyn soverane hevynnys e,
The opposit held of hys chymmys hie,
Cleir schynand bemys, and goldyn symmyris hew,
In laton cullour alteryng haill of new,
Kythyng no syng of heyt be hys vissage,
So neir approchit he his wyntir stage;
Reddy he was to entyr the thrid morn
In clowdy skyis undre Capricorn;
All thocht he be the hart and lamp of hevyn,
Forfeblit wolx hys lemand gylty levyn,   10
Throu the declynyng of hys large round speir.
The frosty regioun ryngis of the yer,
The tyme and sesson bittir, cald and paill,
The schort days that clerkis clepe brumaill,
Quhen brym blastis of the northyn art
Ourquhelmyt had Neptunus in his cart,
And all to schaik the levis of the treis,

129

The rageand storm ourweltrand wally seys.
Ryveris ran reid on spait with watir browne,
And burnys hurlys all thar bankis downe,   20
And landbrist rumland rudely with sik beir,
So lowd ne rumyst wild lyoun or ber;
Fludis monstreis, sik as meirswyne or quhalis,
Fro the tempest law in the deip devalis.
Mars occident, retrograde in his speir,
Provocand stryfe, regnyt as lord that yer;
Rany Oryon with his stormy face
Bewavit oft the schipman by hys race;
Frawart Saturn, chill of complexioun,
Throu quhais aspect darth and infectioun   30
Beyn causyt oft, and mortal pestilens,
Went progressyve the greis of his ascens;
And lusty Hebe, Junoys douchtir gay,
Stude spulyeit of hir office and array.
The soyl ysowpit into watir wak,
The firmament ourcast with rokis blak,
The grond fadyt, and fawch wolx all the feildis,
Montane toppis slekit with snaw ourheildis;
On raggit rolkis of hard harsk quhyn stane
With frosyn frontis cauld clynty clewis schane.   40
Bewte was lost, and barrand schew the landis.
With frostis hair ourfret the feldis standis.
Seir bittir bubbis and the schowris snell
Semyt on the sward a symylitude of hell,
Reducyng to our mynd, in every sted,
Gousty schaddois of eild and grisly ded.
Thik drumly skuggis dyrknyt so the hevyn,
Dym skyis oft furth warpit feirfull levyn,
Flaggis of fire, and mony felloun flaw,
Scharpe soppys of sleit and of the snypand snaw.   50
The dolly dichis war all donk and wait,
The law valle flodderit all with spait,

The plane stretis and every hie way
Full of floschis, dubbis, myre and clay.
Laggerit leyis wallowit farnys schew,
Browne muris kythit thar wysnyt mossy hew,
Bank, bra and boddum blanchit wolx and bar.
For gurl weddir growit bestis hair.
The wynd maid waif the red wed on the dyke,
Bedowyn in donkis deip was every sike.   60
Our craggis and the front of rochis seir
Hang gret ische schouchlis lang as ony speir.
The grond stud barrant, widderit, dosk or gray,
Herbis, flowris and gersis wallowyt away.
Woddis, forrestis, with nakyt bewis blowt,
Stude stripyt of thar weid in every howt.
So bustuusly Boreas his bugill blew,
The deyr full dern doun in the dalis drew;
Smale byrdis, flokkand throu thik ronys thrang,
In chyrmyng and with cheping changit thar sang,   70
Sekand hidlis and hyrnys thame to hyde
Fra feirfull thuddis of the tempestuus tyde;
The watir lynnys rowtis, and every lynd
Quhislit and brayt of the swouchand wynd.
Puyr lauboraris and bissy husband men
Went wait and wery draglit in the fen.
The silly scheip and thar litil hyrd gromys
Lurkis undre le of bankis, woddis, and bromys;
And other dantit gretter bestiall,
Within thar stabillis sesyt into stall,   80
Sik as mulis, horssis, oxin and ky,
Fed tuskyt barys and fat swyne in sty,
Sustenyt war by mannys governance
On hervist and on symmeris purvyance.
Wyde quhar with fors so Eolus schowtis schill
In this congelit sesson scharp and chill,
The callour ayr, penetratyve and puyr,

131

Dasyng the blude in every creatur,
Maid seik warm stovis and beyn fyris hoyt,
In dowbill garmont cled and wily coyt,   90
With mychty drink and metis confortyve,
Agane the stern wyntir forto stryve.
Repatyrrit weil, and by the chymnay bekyt,
At evin be tyme downe a bed I me strekyt,
Warpit my hed, kest on clathis thrynfald,
Fortil expell the peralus persand cald;
I crosyt me, syne bownyt forto sleip,
Quhar, lemand throu the glas, I dyd tak kepe
Latonya, the lang irksum nyght,
Hir subtell blenkis sched and watry lycht,   100
Full hie up quhirlyt in hir regioun,
Till Phebus ryght in oppositioun,
Into the Crab hir proper mansioun draw,
Haldand the hight all thocht the son went law.
Hornyt Hebowd, quhilk we clepe the nycht owle,
Within hir cavern hard I schowt and yowle,
Laithly of form, with crukyt camscho beke,
Ugsum to heir was hir wild elrich screke;
The wild geis claking eik by nyghtis tyde
Atour the cite fleand hard I glyde.   110
On slummyr I slaid full sad, and slepit sound
Quhil the oriyont upwart gan rebound.
Phebus crownyt byrd, the nyghtis orlager,
Clapping his weyngis thrys had crawin cleir;
Approching neir the greking of the day,
Within my bed I walkynnyt quhar I lay;
So fast declynys Synthea the moyn,
And kays keklis on the ruyf aboyn;
Palamedes byrdis crowpyng in the sky,
Fleand on randon, schapyn like ane Y,   120
And as a trumpat rang thar vocis soun,
Quhois cryis bene pronosticatioun

Of wyndy blastis and ventositeis;
Fast be my chalmyr, in heich wysnyt treis,
The soir gled quhislis lowd with mony a pew:
Quhar by the day was dawyn weil I knew,
Bad beit the fyre and the candill alyght,
Syne blissyt me, and in my wedis dyght,
A schot wyndo onschet a litill on char,
Persavyt the mornyng bla, wan and har,   130
With clowdy gum and rak ourquhelmyt the ayr,
The sulye stythly, hasart, rouch and hair,
Branchis bratlyng, and blaknyt schew the brays
With hirstis harsk of waggand wyndill strays,
The dew droppis congelit on stibbill and rynd,
And scharp hailstanys mortfundeit of kynd
Hoppand on the thak and on the causay by.
The schot I closit, and drew inwart in hy,
Chyvirrand for cald, the sesson was so snell,
Schupe with hayt flambe to fleym the fresyng fell   140
And, as I bownyt me to the fyre me by,
Baith up and down the hows I dyd aspy,
And seand Virgill on a lettron stand,
To write onone I hynt a pen in hand,
Fortil perform the poet grave and sad,
Quham sa fer furth or than begun I had,
And wolx ennoyt sum deill in my hart
Thar restit oncompletit sa gret a part.
And to my self I said: 'In gud effect
Thou mon draw furth, the yok lyis on thy nek.'   150
Within my mynde compasyng thocht I so,
Na thing is done quhil ocht remanys ado;
For byssynes, quhilk occurrit on cace,
Ourvolvyt I this volume, lay a space;
And, thocht I wery was, me list not tyre,
Full laith to leif our wark swa in the myre,
Or yit to stynt for bitter storm or rane.

133

Heir I assayt to yok our pleuch agane,
And, as I couth, with afald diligens,
This nixt buke following of profond sentens   160
Has thus begun in the chil wyntir cald,
Quhen frostis doith ourfret baith firth and fald.

(D. F. C. Coldwell, *Selections from Gavin Douglas*)

SIR DAVID LYNDSAY

From *The Dreme*

(i)

Of the Realme of Scotland

Quhen that I had oversene this Regioun,
The quhilk, of nature, is boith gude and fair,
I did propone ane lytill questioun,
Beseikand hir the sam for to declare.
Quhat is the cause our boundis bene so bair?
Quod I: or quhate dois mufe our Miser(i)e?
Or quhareof dois proceid our povertie?

For, throw the supporte of your hie prudence,
Off Scotland I persave the properteis,
And, als, considderis, be experience,   10
Off this countre the gret commoditeis.
First, the haboundance of fyschis in our seis,
And fructual montanis for our bestiall;
And, for our cornis, mony lusty vaill;

The ryche Ryueris, plesand and proffitabyll;
The lustie loochis, with fysche of sindry kyndis;
Hountyng, halkyng, for nobyllis convenabyll;
Forrestis full of Da, Ra, Hartis, and Hyndis;
The fresche fontanis, quhose holesum cristel strandis
Refreschis so the (fair) fluriste grene medis: 20
So laik we no thyng that to nature nedis.

Off euery mettell we have the ryche Mynis,
Baith Gold, Sylver, and stonis precious.
Howbeit we want the Spyces and the Wynis,
Or uther strange fructis delycious,
We have als gude, and more neidfull for us.
Meit, drynk, fyre, clathis, thar my(ch)t be gart abound,
Quhilkis als is nocht in al the Mapamound;

More fairer peple, nor of gretar ingyne,
Nor of more strenth gret dedis tyll indure.   30
Quharefor, I pray yow that ye wald defyne
The principall cause quharefor we ar so pure;
For I marvell gretlie, I yow assure,
Considderand the peple and the ground,
That Ryches suld nocht in this realme redound.

My Sonne, scho said, be my discretioun,
I sall mak answeir, as I understand,
I say to the, under confessioun,
The falt is nocht, I dar weill tak on hand,
Nother in to the peple nor the land.   40
As for the land, it lakis na uther thing
Bot laubour and the pepyllis governyng.

Than quharein lyis our Inprosperitie?
Quod I. I pray yow hartfullie, Madame,
Ye wald declare to me the veritie;
Or quho sall beir of our barrat the blame?
For, be my treuth, to se I thynk gret schame
So plesand peple, and so fair ane land,
And so few verteous dedis tane on hand.

Quod scho: I sall, efter my Jugement,   50
Declare sum causis, in to generall,
And, in to termes schorte, schaw myne intent,

136

And, syne, transcend more in to speciall.
So, this is myne conclusioun fynall:
Wantyng of Justice, polycie, and peace,
Ar cause of thir unhappynes, allace,

It is deficill Ryches tyll incres,
Quhare Polycie makith no residence,
And Policey may never have entres,
Bot quhare that Justice dois delygence   60
To puneis quhare thare may be found offence.
Justice may nocht have Dominatioun,
Bot quhare Peace makis habitatioun.

(S.T.S.(

(ii)

The Complaynt of the Comoun Weill of Scotland

And, thus as we wer talking to and fro,
We saw a boustius berne cum ouir the bent,
But hors, on fute, als fast as he mycht go,
Quhose rayment wes all raggit, rewin, & rent,
With visage leyne, as he had fastit lent:
And fordwart fast his wayis he did advance,
With ane rycht malancolious countynance,

With scrip on hip, and pyikstaff in his hand,
As he had purposit to passe fra hame.
Quod I: gude man, I wald faine understand,   10
Geve that ye plesit, to wyt quhat wer your name.
Quod he: my Sonne, of that I think gret schame;
Bot, sen thow wald of my name have ane feill,
Forsuith, thay call me Ihone the Comoun Weill.

Schir Commoun Weill, quho hes yow so disgysit?
Quod I: or quhat makis yow so miserabyll?
I have marvell to se yow so supprysit,
The quhilk that I have sene so honorabyll.
To all the warld ye have bene proffitabyll,
And weill honorit in everilk Natioun: 20
How happinnis, now, your tribulatioun?

Allace, quod he, thow seis how it dois stand
With me, and quhow I am disherisit
Off all my grace, and mon pas of Scotland,
And go, afore quhare I was cherisit.
Remane I heir, I am bot perysit.
For thare is few to me that takis tent,
That garris me go so raggit, revin, and rent.

My tender friendis ar all put to the flycht;
For polecey is fled agane in France.   30
My Syster, Justice, almaist haith tynt hir sycht,
That scho can nocht hald evinly the ballance.
Plane wrang is plane capitane of Ordinance,
The quhilk debarris Laute and reassoun,
And small remeid is found for oppin treassoun.

In to the south, allace, I was neir slane:
Ouer all the land I culd fynd no releiff;
Almoist betwix the Mers and Lowmabane
I culde nocht knaw ane leill man be ane theif.
To schaw thare reif, thift, murthour, and mischeif,   40
And vecious workis, it wald infect the air:
And, als, langsum to me for tyll declair.

In to the Hieland I could fynd no remeid,
Bot suddantlie I wes put to exile.
Tha sweir swyngeoris thay tuke of me non heid,

Nor amangs thame lat me remane ane quhyle.
Als, in the oute Ylis, and in Argyle,
Unthrift, sweirnes, falset, povertie, and stryfe
Pat polacey in dainger of hir lyfe.

In the Law land I come to seik refuge,   50
And purposit thare to mak my residence.
Bot singulare proffect gart me soune disluge,
And did me gret injuris and offence,
And said to me: swyith, harlote, hy the hence;
And in this countre se thow tak no curis,
So lang as my auctoritie induris.

And now I may mak no langer debait;
Nor I wate nocht quhome to I suld me mene;
For I have socht throw all the Spirituall stait,
Quhilkis tuke na compt for to heir me complene.   60
Thare officiaris, thay held me at disdane;
For Symonie, he rewlis up all that rowte;
And Covatyce, that Carle, gart bar me oute.

Pryde haith chaist (far) frome thame humilitie;
Devotioun is fled unto the freris;
Sensuale plesour hes baneist Chaistitie;
Lordis of Religioun, thay go lyke Seculeris,
Taking more compt in tellyng thare deneris
Nor thay do of thare constitutioun,
Thus ar thay blyndit be ambitioun.   70

Oure gentyll men ar all degenerat(e);
Liberalitie and Lawte, boith, ar loste;
And Cowardyce with Lordis is laureate;
And knychtlie curage turnit in brag and boste;
The Civele weir misgydis ever(ilk) oist.
Thare is nocht ellis bot ilk man for hym self,
That garris me go, thus baneist lyke ane elf.

Tharefor, adew; I may no langer tarye.
Fair weill, quod I, and with sanct Ihone to borrow
Bot, wyt ye weill, my hart was wounder sarye,   80
Quhen Comoun Weill so sopit was in sorrow.
Yit, efter the nycht cumis the glaid morrow;
Quharefor, I pray yow, schaw me, in certane,
Quhen that ye purpose for to cum agane.

That questioun, it sall be sone desydit,
Quod he: thare sall na Scot have confortyng
Off me, tyll that I see the countre gydit
Be wysedome of ane gude auld prudent kyng,   90
Quhilk sall delyte hym maist, abone all thyng,
To put Justice tyll exicutioun,
And on strang tratouris mak puneisioun.

Als yit to the I say ane uther thyng:
I se, rycht weill, that proverbe is full trew,
Wo to the realme that hes ouir young ane king.
With that, he turnit his bak, and said adew.
Ouer firth and fell rycht fast fra me he flew,
Quhose departyng to me was displesand.
With that, Remembrance tuk me be the hand,   100

And sone, me thocht, scho brocht me to the roche,
And to the cove quhare I began to sleip.
With that, one schip did spedalye approche,
Full plesandlie saling apone the deip,
And syne did slake hir salis, and gan to creip
Towart the land, anent quhare that I lay:
Bot, wyt ye weill, I gat ane fellown fraye.

All hir Cannounis sche leit craik of at onis:
Down schuke the stremaris frome the topcastell;
Thay sparit nocht the poulder, nor the stonis;   110

Thay schot thare boltis, & doun *thar* ankeris fell;
The Marenaris, thay did so youte and yell,
That haistalie I stert out of my dreme,
Half in ane fray, and spedalie past hame,

And lychtlie dynit, with lyste and appityte,
Syne efter, past in tyll ane Oritore,
And tuke my pen, and thare began to wryte
All the visioun that I have schawin afore.
Schir, of my dreme as now thou gettis no more,
Bot I beseik God for to send the grace   120
To rewle thy realme in unitie and peace.

From *The Historie of Squyer William Meldrum*

Squire Meldrum at Carrickfergus

For he was wounder amiabill
And in all deidis honorabill,
And ay his honour did avance
In Ingland first and syne in France.
And thair his manheid did assaill
Under the Kingis greit Admirall,
Quhen the greit Navie of Scotland
Passit to the sey aganis Ingland.
And as thay passit be Ireland Coist
The Admirall gart land his Oist,   10
And set Craigfergus into Fyre,
And saifit nouther Barne nor Byre.
It was greit pietie for to heir
Of the pepill the bailfull cheir,
And how the Land folk wer spuilyeit;

Fair wemen underfute wer fuilyeit.
Bot this young Squyer bauld and wicht
Savit all wemen quhair he micht,
All Preistis and Freiris he did save.
Till at the last he did persave   20
Behind ane Garding amiabill
Ane womanis voce richt lamentabill,
And on that voce he followit fast
Till he did see hir at the last
Spuilyeit, nakit as scho was borne.
Twa men of weir wer hir beforne,
Quhilk wer richt cruell men and kene,
Partand the spuilyie thame betwene.
Ane fairer woman nor scho wes
He had not sene in onie place.   30
Befoir him on hir kneis scho fell,
Sayand, for him that heryit Hell,
Help me sweit Sir, I am ane Mayd.
Than softlie to the men he said,
I pray yow give againe hir sark
And tak to yow all uther wark.
Hir Kirtill was of Scarlot reid,
Of gold ane garland of hir heid
Decorit with Enamelyne,
Belt and Brochis of silver fyne.   40
Of yallow Taftais wes hir sark,
Begaryit all with browderit wark
Richt craftelie with gold and silk.
Than said the Ladie quhyte as milk,
Except my sark no thing I crave;
Let thame go hence, with all the lave.
Quod thay to hir, be Sanct Fillane,
Of this ye get nathing agane.
Than said the Squyer courteslie,
Gude Freindis I pray yow hartfullie,   50

Gif ye be worthie Men of Weir
Restoir to hir agane hir Geir;
Or, be greit God that all hes wrocht,
That spuilyie salbe full deir bocht.
Quod thay to him, we the defy,
And drew thair swordis haistely
And straik at him with sa greit Ire
That from his Harnes flew the fyre:
With duntis sa darflie on him dang
That he was never in sic ane thrang.   60
Bot he him manfullie defendit,
And with ane bolt on thame he bendit
And hat the ane upon the heid
That to the ground he fell doun deid:
For to the teith he did him cleif,
Lat him ly thair with ane mischeif.
Than with the uther, hand for hand,
He beit him with his birneist brand:
The uther was baith stout and strang,
And on the Squyer darflie dang.   70
And than the Squyer wrocht greit wonder,
Ay till his sword did shaik in sunder.
Than drew he furth ane sharp dagair,
And did him cleik be the Collair,
And evin in at the collerbane
At the first straik he hes him slane:
He founderit fordward to the ground.
Yit was the Squyer haill and sound:
For quhy, he was sa weill enarmit,
He did escaip fra thame unharmit.   80
And quhen he saw thay wer baith slane
He to that Ladie past agane
Quhair scho stude nakit on the bent,
And said, tak your abulyement;
And scho him thankit full humillie,

143

And put hir claithis on spedilie.
Than kissit he that Ladie fair,
And tuik his leif at hir but mair.
Be that the Taburne and Trumpet blew,
And everie man to shipburd drew.   90
That Ladie was dolent in hart,
From tyme scho saw he wald depart
That hir relevit from hir harmes,
And hint the Squyer in hir armes
And said, will ye byde in this Land,
I sall yow tak to my Husband.

(S.T.S. I)

RICHARD MAITLAND

On the New Yeir 1560

In this new yeir I sie bot weir;
Na caus to sing.
In this new yeir I sie bot weir;
Na caus thair is to sing.

I cannot sing for the vexatioun
Of Frenchmen, and the Congregatioun,
That hes maid troubil in the natioun,
And monye bair bigging.
    In this new yeir, etc.

I have na will to sing or dans   **10**
For feir of England and of France.
God send thame sorrow and mischance
In caus of thair cuming.
    In this new yeir, etc.

We ar sa reulit, riche and puir,
That we wait not quhair to be suire,
The bordour as the Borrow muir,
Quhair sum perchance will hing.
    In this new yeir, etc.

And yit I think it best that we   **20**
Pluck up our hairt, and mirrie be.
For thoch we wald ly doun and die,
It will us helpe na thing.
    In this new yeir, etc.

Lat us pray God to staunche this weir;
That we may leif withoutin feir,
In mirrines, quhil we ar heir:
And hevin at our ending.
　　In this new yeir, etc.

(Pinkerton, *Ancient Scotish Poems*)

Satire on the Age

Quhair is the blythnes that hes bein
Bayth in burgh and landwart sein
Amang lordis and ladeis schein;
Dansing, singing, game and play?
Bot weill I wait nocht quhat thay mein:
All merrines is worne away.

For nou I heir na wourde of Yule
In kirk, on cassay, nor in skuil.
Lordis lat thair kitchings cule
And drawis thame to the Abbay:　　　　　10
And scant hes ane to keip their mule.
All houshalding is worne away.

I saw no gysars all this yeir,
Bot kirkmen cled as men of weir;
That nevir cummis in the quheir;
Lyk ruffians' is thair array:
To preitche and teitche, that will not leir.
The kirk gudis thai waste away.

Kirkmen, affoir, war gude of lyf;
Preitchit, teitchit, and staunchit stryf.　　　20
Thai feirit nother swerd nor knyf

For luif of God, the suith to say.
All honorit thame, bayth man and wyf;
Devotioun wes nocht away.

Our faders wys war, and discreit;
Thai had bayth honour, men and meit.
With luif thai did thair tennents treit;
And had aneuch in press to lay.
Thai wantit nother malt nor quheit,
And merrines was nocht away.   30

And we hald nother Yule nor Pace,
Bot seik our meit from place to place.
And we have nother luck nor grace,
We gar our landis dowbil pay:
Our tennents cry 'alace, alace,
That reuth and petie is away!'

Now we have mair, it is weill kend,
Nor our forbearis had to spend;
Bot far les at the yeiris end,
And never hes ane merie day.   40
God will na ryches to us send
Sa lang as honour is away.

We waist far mair now, lyk vane fulis,
We and our page, to turse our mulis,
Nor thai did than, that held grit Yulis,
Of meit and drink said never nay.
Thai had lang formes quhair we have stulis,
And merrines wes nocht away.

Of our wanthrift sum wytis playis,
And sum thair wantoun vane arrayis;   50
Sum the wyt on thair wyfis layis

That in the court wald gang sa gay,
And care nocht quha the merchand payis,
Quhil pairt of land be put away.

The kirkmen keipis na professioun;
The temporall men commits oppressioun,
Puttand the puir from thair possessioun—
Na kynd of feir of God have thai.
Thai cummar bayth the court and sessioun
And chasis charitie away.   60

Quhen ane of thame sustenis wrang,
We cry for justice heid, and hang;
Bot quhen our neichbours we our-gang
We lawbour justice to delay.
Affectioun blindis us sa lang
All equitie is put away.

To mak actis we have sum feil:
God wait gif that we keip thame weill
We cum to bar with jak o steil
As we wald boist the juge and 'fray: 70
Of sic justice I have na skeil,
Quhair rewle and order is away.

Our lawis ar lichtleit for abusioun;
Sumtyme is clokit with colusioun,
Quhik causis of blude grit effusioun,
For na man sparis now to slay.
Quhat bringis cuntries to confusioun
Bot quhair that justice is away?

Quha is to wyte, quha can schaw us?
Quha bot our nobils, that suld knaw us   80
And till honorabil deidis draw us?

Lat never comoun weil decay,
Or els sum mischief will befaw us,
And nobilnes we put away.

Put our awn laws to executioun;
Upon trespasses mak punitioun;
To crewel folk seik na remissioun;
For peax and justice lat us pray,
In dreid sum strange new institutioun
Cum, and our custome put away.   90

Amend your lyvis, ane and all,
Els bewar of ane suddane fall:
And pray to God that maid us all
To send us joy that lestis ay,
And lat us nocht to sin be thrall
Bot put all vyce and wrang away.

(Pinkerton, *Ancient Scotish Poems*)

? JAMES V

Chrystis Kirk on the Grene

Was never in Scotland hard nor sene
Sic dansing nor deray,
Nother in Falkland on the grene,
Nor Peblis to the play,
As was of wowaris as I wene
At Chrystis kirk on ane day.
Thair come our kittie wesching clene
In hir new kirtill of gray,
Full gay,
At Chrystis kirk on the grene.   10

To dance the damisallis thame dicht,
And lassis licht of laittis;
Thair gluvis war of the raffell richt;
Thair schone war of the straitis:
Thair kirtillis war of the lincum licht
Weill prest with mony plaitis.
Thay war so nyce quhen men tham nicht
Thay squeild lyk ony gaitis,
Ful loud
At Chrystis kirk on the grene.   20

Sche scornit Jok and scrippit at him,
And morgeound him with mokkis;
He wald have luffit hir; sche wald nocht lat him,
For all his yallow lokkis;
He cherist hir; scho bad ga chat him,

Sche comptit him nocht tua clokkis;
Sa schamfullie ane schort goun sat him,
His lymmis was lyk twa rokkis,
Sche said
At Chrystis kirk on the grene.   30

Off all thir madinis myld as meid,
Was nane sa gymp as Gillie;
As ony rose hir rude was reid,
Hir lyre was lyk the lillie;
Bot yallow yallow was hir heid,
And sche of luif so sillie,
Thocht all hir kin suld have bein deid,
Sche wald have bot sweit Willie,
Allane,
At Chrystis kirk on the grein.   40

Stevin come steppand in with stendis,
No renk mycht him arrest;
Platfut he bobbit up with bendis,
For Mald he maid requeist;
He lap quhill he lay on his lendis,
Bot rysand he was prest
Quhill he hostit at bayth the endis
In honour of the feist
That day
At Chrystis kirk on the grein.   50

Thome Lutar was thair menstrale meit;
O Lord, gif he culd lance!
He playit so schill and sang so sweit
Quhill Towsie tuik ane trance;
All auld lycht futtis he did forleyt
And counterfutit France;
He him avysit as man discreit

151

And up the moreis dance
Scho tuik
At Chrystis kirk on the grein. 60

Than Robene Roy begouth to revell,
And Dowie to him druggit;
'Lat be!' quod Johke, and callit him gavell,
And be the taill him tuggit;
He turnit and cleikit to the cavell,
Bot Lord than gif thai luggit!
Thai partit thair play thane with ane nevell
Men wait gif hair wes ruggit
Betwene thame
At Chrystis kirk on the grein. 70

Ane bend ane bow, sic sturt couth steir him;
Grit scayth war to have scard him;
He chesit ane flaine as did affeir him;
The tother said dirdum dardum;
Throw bayth the cheikis he thocht to cheir him,
Or throw the chaftis have charde him
Bot be ane myle it come nocht neir him
I can nocht say quhat mard him
Thair
At Chrystis kirk on the grein. 80

With that ane freynd of his cryit, fy!
And up ane arow drew,
He forgeit it so ferslye
The bow in flenders flew;
Sa was the will of God, trow I;
For had the tre bene trew,
Men said that kend his archerie
That he had slane anew

152

That day
At Chrystis kirk on the grein.   90

Ane haistie hensour callit Harie,
Quhilk wes ane archer heynd,
Tit up ane takill but ony tarye,
That turment so him teynd;
I wait nocht quhidder his hand cud varie,
Or gif the man was his freynd,
Bot he chapit throw the michtis of Marie
As man that na evill meynd
That tyme
At Chrystis kirk on the grein.   100

Than Lowrie as ane lyoun lap,
And sone ane flane culd fedder;
He hecht to pers him at the pape,
Thairon to wed ane wedder;
He hit him on the wambe ane wap,
And it bust lyk ane bledder;
Bot lo! as fortoun was and hap,
His doublat was of ledder
And sauft him
At Chrystis kirk on the grein.   110

The baff so boustuousle abasit him,
To the erd he duschit doun;
The tother for dreid he preissit him
And fled out of the toun;
The wyffis come furth and up thay paisit him
And fand lyff in the loun
And with thre routis thay raisit him
And coverit him of swoune
Agane
At Chrystis kirk on the grein.   120

Ane yaip young man that stude him neist
Lousit of ane schot with ire;
He etlit the berne evin in the breist,
The bout flew our the byre;
Ane cryit that he had slane ane preist
Ane myle beyond ane myre;
Than bow and bag fra him he caist,
And fled als fers as fyre,
Of flint
At Chrystis kirk on the grein.   130

With forkis and flalis thay leit grit flappis,
And flang togither with friggis
With bougaris of barnis thai birst blew cappis,
Quhill thay of bernis maid briggis;
The rerde rais rudlie with the rappis,
Quhen rungis was layd on riggis;
The wyffis come furth with cryis and clappis
'Lo quhair my lyking liggis,'
Quod scho
At Chrystis kirk on the grein.   140

Thay girnit and leit gird with granis;
Ilk gossop uther grevit;
Sum straikit stingis, sum gadderit stanis,
Sum fled and weill eschewit;
The menstrale wan within ane wanis;
That day full weill he previt,
For he come hame with unbrisde banis,
Quhair fechtaris war mischevit
For ever
At Chrystis kirk on the grein.   150

Heich Huchoun with ane hissill rys
To red can throw thame rummill;

154

He mudlit thame doun lyk ony myse,
He wes na baty bummill.
Thocht he wes wicht he wes nocht wys,
With sic Iatouris to geummill.
For fra his thoume thay dang ane sklys
Quhill he cryit barlaw fummill
Ouris
At Chrystis kirk on the grein.   160

Quhen that he saw his blude so reid,
To fle micht no man lat him;
He wend it had bene for ald feid,
The far sarar it sat him;
He gart his feit defend his heid;
He thocht thay cryit have at him,
Quhill he was past out of all pleid—
He suld be swyft that gat him
Throw speid
At Chrystis kirk on the grein.   170

The toun soutar in breif was boudin;
His wyf hang in his waist;
His body was in blude all browdin;
He granit lyk ony gaist;
Hir g(l)itterand hairis that war full goldin,
So hard in luif him laist
That for hir saik he wes unyoldin
Sevin myle quhen he wes chaist
And mair
At Chrystis kirk on the grein.   180

The millar was of manlie mak;
To meit him was na mowis;
Thair durst na ten cum him to tak
So nobbit he thair nowis.

155

The buschement haill about him brak
And bickert him with bowis,
Syn tratourlie behind his bak
Ane hewit him on the howis
Behind
At Chrystis kirk on the grein.   190

Twa that was herdismen of the herde
Ran upone uther lyk rammis;
Thai forsy freikis richt uneffeird
Bet on with barow trammis;
Bot quhair thair gobbis war bayth ungird,
Thai gat upon the gammis,
Quhill bludie barkit was thair berd,
As thay had worreit lambis
Most lyk
At Chrystis kirk on the grein.   200

The wyffis cast up ane hidduous yell,
Quhen all the youngkeiris yokkit;
Als fers as ony fyr flauchtis fell
Freikis to the feild thai flokit;
Thay cavellis with clubbis culd uther quell,
Quhill blude at breistis out bokkit;
So rudlie rang the Commoun bell
Quhill all the steipill rokkit
For rerde
At Chrystis Kirk on the grein.   210

Quhen thai had beirit lyk batit bullis,
And brane wode brynt in balis,
Thai wox als mait as ony mulis,
That maggit war with malis,
For fantnes thay forfochin fulis
Fell doun lyk flauchter falis;

Fresche men com hame and halit the dulis,
And dang thame doun in dalis
Bedene
At Chrystis kirk on the grein.   220

Quhen all wes done, Dic with ane ax
Come furth to fell ane futher;
Quod he, 'Quhair ar yon hangit smaikis
Richt now that hurt my brother?'
His wyf bad him gang hame gud glaikis
And swa did Meg his mother,
He turnit and gaif thame bath thair paikis,
For he durst stryk na uther,
Men said
At Chrystis kirk on the grene.   230

finis.

(Maitland Folio MS., I, S.T.S.)

ANONYMOUS

Quhen Flora had ourfret the firth
In May, of every moneth quene,
Quhen merle and mavis singis with mirth,
Sweit melling in the schawis schene,
Quhen all luvaris rejosit bene,
And most desyrus of thair pray,
I hard a lusty luvar mene,
'I luve, bot I dar nocht assay.

Strang ar the panis I daylie prufe,
Bot yit with pacience I sustene,   10
I am so fetterit with the lufe
Onlie of my lady schene,
Quhilk for hir bewty mycht be quene,
Natour so craftely alwey
Hes done depaint that sweit serene:
Quhome I luf, I dar nocht assay.

Scho is so brycht of hyd and hew,
I lufe bot hir allone, I wene;
Is non hir luf that may eschew
That blenkis of that dulce amene,   20
So cumly cleir at hir twa ene,
That scho ma luvaris dois effrey
Than evir of Grice did fair Helene;
Quhom I luve, I dar nocht assay.'

(*Bannatyne MS*, III)

My Hairt is Heich Aboif

My hairt is heich aboif, my body is full of blis,
For I am sett in lufe als weill as I wald wis.
I lufe my lady pure and scho luvis me agane;
I am hir serviture, scho is my soverane;
Scho is my verry harte, I am hir howp and heill;
Scho is my joy inwart, I am hir luvar leill;
I am hir bound and thrall, scho is at my command;
I am perpetuall hir man both fute and hand.
The thing that may hir pleis, my body sall fulfill;
Quhatevir hir diseis, it dois my body ill.   10
My bird, my bony ane, my tendir bab venust,
My lufe, my lyfe allane, my liking and my lust,
We interchange our hairtis in utheris armis soft;
Spreitles we twa depairtis, usand our luvis oft.
We murne quhen licht day dawis; we plene the nycht is schort;
We curs the cok that crawis that hinderis our disport.
I glowffin up agast quhen I hir mys on nycht,
And in my oxster fast I find the bowster richt.
Than langour on me lyis, lyk Morpheus, the mair,
Quhilk causis me uprys and to my sweit repair,   20
And than is all the sorrow furth of remembrance,
That evir I had a forrow in luvis observance.
Thus nevir I do rest, so lusty a lyfe I leid
Quhen that I list to test the well of womanheid.
Luvaris in pane, I pray God send yow sic remeid
As I haif nycht and day, yow to defend frome deid.
Thairfoir be evir trew unto your ladeis fre,
And thay will on yow rew, as mine hes done one me.

(*Bannatyne MS*, III)

The Reid in the Loch Sayis

Thocht raging stormes movis us to schaik,
And wind makis waters us overflow,
We yeild thairto bot dois not brek,
And in the calme bent up we grow.

So baneist men, thocht princes raige,
And prisoners be not disparit,
Abyde the calm quhill that it suaige;
For tyme sic caussis hes reparit.

(Maitland Quarto MS)

ALEXANDER SCOTT

Quha is perfyte

Quha is perfyte
To put in wryt
The inwart murnyng & mischance,
Or to indyte
The grit delyte
Of lustie lufis obscherwance,
    Bot he that may certane
    Patiently suffir pane,
    To wyn his souerane
        In recompance.   10

Albeid I knaw
Of luvis law
The plesour & the panis smart,
    Yit I stand aw
    For to furthschaw
The quyet secreitis of my harte;
    For it may fortoun raith,
    To do hir body skaith,
    Quhilk wait that of thame baith
        I am expert.   20

Scho wait my wo
That is ago—
Scho wait my weilfair and remeid—
    Scho wait also
    I lufe no mo

Bot hir—the well of womanheid;
    Scho wait withouttin faill
    I am hir luvar laill;
    Scho hes my hairt alhaill
        Till I be deid.   30

    That bird of bliss
    In bewty is
In erd the only A per se,
    Quhais mowth to kiss
    Is worth, I wiss,
The warld full of gold to me;
    Is nocht in erd I cure,
    Bot pleiss my lady pure,
    Syne be hir scheruiture
        Vnto I de.   40

    Scho is my lufe;
    At hir behufe
My hairt is subiect, bound & thrall;
    For scho dois moif
    My hairt aboif,
To se hir proper persoun small.
    Sen scho is wrocht at will,
    That natur may fulfill,
    Glaidly I gif hir till
        Body and all.   50

    Thair is nocht wie
    Can estimie
My sorrow and my sichingis sair;
    For I am so
    Done fathfullie
In faworis with my lady fair.
    That baith our hairtis ar ane.

Luknyt in luvis chene,
And evirilk greif is gane
For evir mair.   60

(S.T.S.)

To luve unluvit

To luve unluvit it is ane pane;
For scho that is my souerane,
    Sum wantoun man so he hes set hir,
That I can get no lufe agane,
    Bot brekis my hairt, & nocht the bettir.

Quhen that I went with that sweit may,
To dance, to sing, to sport and pley,
    And oft tymes in my armis plet hir;
I do now mvrne both nycht & day,
    And brekis my hart, & nocht the bettir.   10

Quhair I wes wont to se hir go
Rycht trymly passand to and fro,
    With cumly smylis quhen that I met hir;
And now I leif in pane & wo,
    And brekis [my hairt, and nocht the bettir].

Quhattane ane glaikit fule am I
To slay myself with malancoly,
    Sen weill I ken I may nocht get hir!
Or quhat suld be the caus, and quhy,
    To brek [my hairt, and nocht the bettir]?   20

My hairt, sen thow may nocht hir pleiss,
Adew, as gude lufe cumis as gaiss,
    Go chuss ane udir and forget hir;

163

God gif him dolour and diseiss
That brekis thair hairt and nocht the bettir.

(Quod Scot quen his wyf left him.)
(S.T.S.)

A Rondel of Luve

Lo! quhat it is to lufe,
Lerne ye, that list to prufe,
Be me, I say, that no wayis may
The grund of greif remufe,
Bot still decay, both nycht and day:
Lo! quhat it is to lufe.

Lufe is ane fervent fyre,
Kendillit without desyre:
Schort plesour, lang displesour;
Repentence is the hyre;   10
Ane pure tressour without mesour:
Lufe is ane fervent fyre.

To lufe and to be wyiss,
To rege with gud adwyiss,
Now thus, now than, so gois the game,
Incertane is the dyiss:
Thair is no man, I say, that can
Both lufe and to be wyiss.

Fle alwayis frome the snair;
Lerne at me to be ware;   20
It is ane pane and dowbill trane
Of endles wo and cair;
For to refrane that denger plane,
Fle alwayis frome the snair.

(S.T.S.)

ALEXANDER MONTGOMERIE

The Nicht is Neir Gone

Hay! now the day dawis;
The jolie Cok crawis;
Now shroudis the shawis,
　Throw Natur anone.
The thissell-cok cryis
On lovers wha lyis.
Now skaillis the skyis:
　The nicht is neir gone.

The feildis overflowis
With gowans that growis,　　　　　10
Quhair lilies lyk low is,
　Als rid as the rone.
The turtill that trew is,
With nots that renewis,
Hir pairtie persewis:
　The nicht is neir gone.

Now Hairtis with Hyndis,
Conforme to thair kyndis,
Hie tursis thair tyndis,
　On grund whair they grone.　　　20
Now Hurchonis, with Hairis,
Ay passis in pairis;
Quhilk deuly declaris
　The nicht is neir gone.

165

The sesone excellis
Thrugh sweetnes that smellis;
Now Cupid compellis
　　Our hairtis echone
On Venus wha waikis,
To muse on our maikis,　　　　　　　　　　　30
Syn sing, for thair saikis:—
　　The nicht is neir gone.

All curageous knichtis
Aganis the day dichtis
The breist plate that bright is,
　　To feght with thair fone.
The stoned steed stampis
Throw curage and crampis,
Syn on the land lampis:
　　The nicht is neir gone.　　　　　　　　　40

The freikis on feildis
That wight wapins weildis
With shyning bright shieldis
　　As Titan in trone:
Stiff speiris in reistis,
Over cursoris creistis,
Ar brok on thair breistis:
　　The nicht is neir gone.

So hard ar thair hittis,
Some sweyis, some sittis,　　　　　　　　　50
And some perforce flittis
　　On grund whill they grone.
Syn groomis that gay is,
On blonkis that brayis,
With swordis assayis:
　　The nicht is neir gone.

　　　　　　　　　　　　　　　　　　(S.T.S.)

166

Off the Cherry and the Slae (opening stanzas)

About ane bank, quhair birdis on bewis
Ten thousand tymes thair nottis renewis
   Ilk hour into the day,
Quhair merle and mavis micht be sene,
With progne and with phelomene,
   Quhilk causit me to Stay.
I lay and lentt me to ane buss,
   To heir the birdis beir;
Thair mirth was so melodius
   Throw nature of the yeir: 10
     Sum singing, sum springing,
       So heich into the skye;
    So nimlie and trimlie
     Thir birdis flew me by.

I saw the hurchun and the hair,
Quhilk fed amange the flouris fair,
   War happin to and fro:
I saw the cunyng and the kat,
Quhais downis with the dew was wat,
   With mony beistis ma.   20
The hairt, the hynd, the da, the rae,
   The fumart and the fox,
Was skippin all frome bray to bray
   Amang the watter brokis;
     Sum feidding, sum dreidding,
       In cais of suddane snairis;
    With skipping, and trippin,
     Thay hanttit ay in pairis.

The air was so attemperat,
But ony mist Immaculatt, 30
Baith purefeit and cleir;
The feildis ower all was flureischit,
As natour haid thame nurischitt,
Bayth delicat and deir:
And everie blume on branche and bewch
So prettilie thay spred,
Hingand thair heidis out ower the heuch,
In mayis cullour cled;
Sum knapping, Sum drapping
Of balmie liquor sweit, 40
Destelling and smelling
Throw phebus helsum heit.

The Coukou and the cussatt cryid,
The turtill on the uther syde,
Na plesure haid to play:
Sua schill in sorow was hir sang
That with hir voce the rochis rang,
For echo ansuerit ay,
Lamenting still Narcissus' cais,
That stervit at the well; 50
Quha throw the schadow of his face
For luif did slay him sell:
Sair weiping and creiping
About that well he baid;
Quhylis lying, quhylis crying,
Bot it na ansuer maid.

The dew as dyamontis did hing
Upoun the tender twiskis ying,
Owertwinkling all the treis:
And ay quhair flouris did flureis fair, 60
Thair suddanlie I saw repair

168

Ane suarme of sounding beis.
Sum sueitlie hes the hony socht
   Quhill thay war claggit soir;
Sum willinglie the walx hes wrocht
   To keip it up in store;
     So heiping, for keiping
       Into thair hyvis thay hyd it:
     Preciselie and wiselie
       For winter thay provydit.   70

To pen the plesure of that park
How everie blaysum, brench and bark
   Aganis the sone did schyne,
I leave to poyetis to compyle
In staitlie verss and ornate style:
   It passis my ingyne.
Bot as I movit me allone,
   I saw ane rever Rin
Out ouer ane craig and Roch of stone,
   Syne lichtit in ane lin: 80
     With tumbling and Rumbling
       Among the rockis round,
     Devalling and falling
       Into the pitt profound.

(Laing MS, in S.T.S. Supplement to Poems, 1910)

To his Maistres

So swete a kis yistrene fra thee I reft,
In bowing down thy body on the bed,
That evin my lyfe within thy lippis I left;
Sensyne from thee my spirits wald never shed;

To folow thee it from my body fled,
And left my corps als cold as ony kie.
Bot when the danger of my death I dred,
To seik my spreit I sent my harte to thee;
Bot it wes so inamored with thyn ee,
With thee it myndit likwyse to remane: 10
So thou hes keepit captive all the thrie,
More glaid to byde then to returne agane.
Except thy breath thare places had suppleit,
Even in thyn armes, thair doutles had I deit.

(S.T.S.)

The Solsequium

    Lyk as the dum
    Solsequium,
    With cair ouercum,
And sorow, when the sun goes out of sight,
    Hings doun his head,
    And droups as dead,
    And will not spread,
Bot louks his leavis throu langour of the nicht,
    Till folish Phaeton ryse,
      With whip in hand,   10
    To cleir the cristall skyis,
      And light the land:
    Birds in thair bour
    Luiks for that hour,
And to thair prince ane glaid good-morow givis;
    Fra thyn, that flour
    List not to lour,
Bot laughis on Phoebus lousing out his leivis:

    So fairis with me,
    Except I be   20

Whair I may se
My lamp of licht, my Lady and my Love.
　　Fra scho depairts,
　　Ten thousand dairts,
　　In syndrie airts,
Thirlis throu my hevy hart, but rest or rove;
　　My countenance declairs
　　　My inward grief;
　　Good hope almaist dispairs
　　　To find relief.　　　　　　　　　　30
　　　I die—I dwyn—
I loth on eviry thing I look—alace!
　　Till Titan myne
　　Upon me shyne,
That I revive throu favour of hir face.

　　Fra she appeir
　　Into hir spheir,
　　Begins to cleir
The dawing of my long desyrit day:
　　Then Curage cryis　　　　　　　　　　40
　　On Hope to ryse,
　　Fra he espyis
My noysome nicht of absence worne away.
　　No wo, when I awalk,
　　　May me impesh;
　　Bot, on my staitly stalk,
　　　I florish fresh.
　　I spring—I sprout—
　　My leivis ly out—
My colour changes in ane hartsum hew.　　50
　　No more I lout,
　　Bot stands up stout,
As glade of hir, for whom I only grew.

O happie day!
Go not away.
Apollo! stay
Thy chair from going doun into the west:
Of me thou mak
Thy zodiak,
That I may tak   60
My plesur, to behold whom I love best.
Thy presence me restores
    To lyf from death;
Thy absence also shores
    To cut my breath.
I wish, in vane,
Thee to remane,
Sen primum mobile sayis alwayis nay;
At leist thy wane
Turn soon agane.   70
Fareweill, with patience perforce, till day.

(S.T.S.)

ALEXANDER HUME

Of the Day Estivall

O perfite light, quhilk schaid away,
The darkenes from the light,
And set a ruler ou'r the day,
Ane uther ou'r the night.

Thy glorie when the day foorth flies,
Mair vively dois appeare,
Nor at midday unto our eyes,
The shining Sun is cleare.

The schaddow of the earth anon,
Remooves and drawes by,   10
Sine in the East, when it is gon,
Appeares a clearer sky.

Quhilk Sunne perceaves the little larks,
The lapwing and the snyp,
And tunes their sangs like natures clarks,
Ou'r midow, mure, and stryp.

Bot everie bais'd nocturnall beast,
Na langer may abide,
They hy away baith maist and least,
Them selves in howis to hide.   20

They dread the day fra thay it see,
And from the sight of men.

To saits, and covars fast they flee,
As Lyons to their den.

Oure Hemisphere is poleist clein,
And lightened more and more,
While everie thing be clearely sein,
Quhilk seemed dim before.

Except the glistering astres bright,
Which all the night were cleere,   30
Offusked with a greater light,
Na langer dois appeare.

The golden globe incontinent,
Sets up his shining head,
And ou'r the earth and firmament,
Displayes his beims abread.

For joy the birds with boulden throts,
Agains his visage shein,
Takes up their kindelie musicke nots,
In woods and gardens grein.   40

Up braids the carefull husbandman,
His cornes, and vines to see,
And everie tymous artisan,
In buith works busilie.

The pastor quits the slouthfull sleepe,
And passis forth with speede,
His little camow-nosed sheepe,
And rowtting kie to feede.

The passenger from perrels sure,
Gangs gladly foorth the way: 50

174

Breife, everie living creature,
Takes comfort of the day,

The subtile mottie rayons light,
At rifts thay are in wonne,
The glansing thains, and vitre bright,
Resplends against the sunne.

The dew upon the tender crops,
Lyke pearles white and round,
Or like to melted silver drops,
Refreshes all the ground.   60

The mystie rocke, the clouds of raine,
From tops of mountaines skails,
Cleare are the highest hils and plaine,
The vapors takes the vails.

Begaried is the saphire pend,
With spraings of skarlet hew,
And preciously from end till end,
Damasked white and blew.

The ample heaven of fabrik sure,
In cleannes dois surpas,   70
The chrystall and the silver pure,
Or clearest poleist glas.

The time sa tranquill is and still,
That na where sall ye find,
Saife on ane high, and barren hill,
Ane aire of peeping wind.

(S.T.S.)

MARK ALEXANDER BOYD

Sonet of Venus and Cupid

Fra banc to banc, fra wod to wod, I rin
Ourhailit with my feble fantasie,
Lyc til a leif that fallis from a trie
Or til a reid ourblawin with the wind.
Twa gods gyds me: the ane of tham is blind,
Ye, and a bairn brocht up in vanitie;
The nixt a wyf ingenrit of the se,
And lichter nor a dauphin with hir fin.

Unhappie is the man for evirmaire
That teils the sand and sawis in the aire;   10
Bot twyse unhappier is he, I lairn,
That feidis in his hairt a mad desyre,
And follows on a woman throw the fyre,
Led be a blind and teichit be a bairn.

(MS, National Library of Scotland)

176

BIOGRAPHICAL NOTES

JAMES THE FIRST was born at Dunfermline. He was the second son of Robert the Third and Queen Annabella. The age and infirmity of King Robert caused him to trust the kingdom to his brother, the Duke of Albany, who tried to get the crown by murdering his nephew David, the heir to the throne. As a result, James, now the only obstacle between Albany and the throne, was sent to France for safety in 1405. The ship bearing him to the court of Charles the Sixth was intercepted by the English, although Scotland and England were not at that time at war, and the young prince, then in his eleventh year, was held prisoner until 1424 in England. He was then sold back to the Scots as their king for a ransom of £40,000. He was the best of the Stewart kings, a fine poet well read in European poetry and particularly under the spell of Chaucer. He married Lady Jane (or Joan) Beaufort, the heroine of his *Kingis Quair*.

Of ROBERT HENRYSOUN or HENDERSOUN, as of most of these makars, very little is known. Dunbar in his *Lament* mentions his death in Dunfermline. In the Chartulary of Dunfermline Abbey there are three deeds relating to the years 1477–1478 which are witnessed by a *Magister Robertus Henryson, notarius publicus*. Dunbar in his poem also calls him 'Maister', which was the title of an M.A. at the time—Dunbar's poem was written *circa* 1506. There are various traditions of the poet, but none verifiable. One is that he died of a flux, laughing at a spaewife who tried to cure him, and making a rude joke at her expense. Another is that he was a schoolmaster, or choirmaster at Dunfermline Abbey. Although he was clearly a highly educated man and was called Master, his name does not appear in the lists of St. Andrews, the only university in Scotland at the time, so he must have graduated abroad, probably at Paris, which was to Scotland then very nearly what London is now, culturally speaking. Glasgow University was founded in 1451 and in 1462 the name 'venerable Master Robert Henrysoun, licentiate in Arts and Bachelor in Decrees' appears among the incorporated members. He has been mentioned as father of the Lord Justice Clerk who fell with James the Fourth at Flodden—the illegitimate one if, as is almost certain, he was a cleric. That is as much as can be said about his life. From his poems we can deduce that he lived to a considerable age, that he was of a serene and humorous temperament, that he alone of the makars was really comparable with Chaucer in breadth, humanity, balance of mind, humour, learning (here he is surpassed by Gawin Douglas) and temperament. He has elements of true greatness easily borne, and his *Testament of Cresseid* is to my mind the finest of Scots poems to this day—a truly noble work of poetic genius by the man who, more than any other poet, was the spiritual forebear of Burns, who has much of his large, humane geniality. He left behind him a mass of other fine poetry which has been best edited so far by Gregory Smith for the Scottish Texts Society, and by H. Harvey Wood in a students' edition.

Of WALTER KENNEDY even less is known, and almost nothing of his has come down to us. He lived at the court of James the Fourth and was a rival of Dunbar, with whom he engaged in a poetic duel of scurrilous denunciation called *The Flyting of Dunbar and Kennedy*. He was a Gael from the west coast, and on the evidence of the flyting he was every bit as technically competent a poet as Dunbar, but of rather coarser grain. He seems to have been related to the king, and it is known that he bought a house at Glentig in the year 1504. Dunbar mentions him in his *Lament* as being at point of death. The poem here given is found in the Bannatyne Manuscript, which together with two or three other such home-made anthologies (the Maitland MS, Maitland Quarto, Asloan Manuscript, Reidpeth Manuscript and one or two others) is the main source, almost the only source, of such medieval Scots poetry as has come down to us —a small proportion we may be sure, but probably including much of the best.

WILLIAM DUNBAR, in some ways the greatest (technically and imaginatively) and certainly the most original of these makars, we know a little more about. He was a courtier of some sort of James the Fourth's, in what capacity we don't know—probably various capacities. Half-a-dozen or so of his poems were printed during his lifetime by Chepman and Myller of Edinburgh in 1508—the first work of printed literature in Scotland. He travelled abroad on unspecified court business, and in his youth also perhaps as a friar or novice. In August 1500 he was awarded a pension of £10 per annum for life, paid by the king, subject to withdrawal if he should receive a benefice worth £40 per annum. In November 1507 this was increased to £20, and in August 1510 to £80, subject to withdrawal if he received a church benefice of £100 or more. There is a reference to a payment of an offering of seven French crowns by the king on 14 March 1503 (the year of James's marriage) as 'the kingis offerand at Maister William Dunbar's first mes (mass)' which suggests that he was an ordained priest. Kennedy has much to say about his family in the *Flyting*, but no great credence can be given to a poem in which exaggeration and lies are of the essence, defamation of character the object. There is a reference in

178

the registers of St. Andrews univeristy to a William Dunbar studying there—it is highly probable that he took his degree there. But that is all that can safely be said of Dunbar, though conjecture, rumour, tradition has added much else—that he met Villon in France (impossible as Villon disappeared three years after Dunbar's likely birth-date) and much else. That he was either a younger son of a landed family or an illegitimate one is certain. He tells us himself that his nurse called him 'bishop' when he was an infant—that he was destined, like younger sons and their ilk, for the church. That he was smallish, stocky, nimble, emerges from the poems: also that he was normally of a gay and extrovert temper, but subject to fits of acute depression bordering on melancholy, brooding over his wrongs (and they were many and severe, bordering on degradation, considering his genius and great gifts), and raging against his oppressors. He was fiery, mercurial, subtle of mind, devious, complicated, of powerful practical intellect rather than the contemplative philosophical kind, sexually repressed (as we would say) and neurotic, partly owing to the vows of celibacy exacted from a clergyman, partly owing to his own nature.

Before Dunbar, the long poem was the staple of Scots art-poetry: he left a body of short poems in lyric form which for sheer range and variety has never been excelled: he was an incomparable master of verse and language, yet so far from being a mere technician with little to say, the urgency of what he has to say often strains the fabric to breaking-point. In terms of Scottish poetry he was at once the last of the medievals and the first of the moderns: with him the romance tradition of feudal chivalry passes and the realist tradition of the bourgeoisie is ushered in, though no man was less of a 'bourgeois'. His class, however, the lower landed gentry, had common cause with bourgeois political aims in Scotland. If Burns and Henrysoun have natural affinities, the modern counterpart of Dunbar is C. M. Grieve (Hugh MacDiarmid).

GAWIN DOUGLAS, bishop of Dunkeld and a younger contemporary of Dunbar, was of the powerful baronial family of that name. He was the third son of Archibald Douglas, Earl of Angus, famous to school histories as 'Bell the Cat'. He may have been born at Tantallon Castle looking over to the Bass Rock, or at Dudhope near Dundee, or Abernethy—all Douglas residences. He took his degree at St. Andrews in 1494, and probably finished at Paris and other continental universities. Douglas at once gained the kind of preferment sought in vain by Dunbar, the king giving him the teinds of Monymusk when he was but twenty-one, then the parsonage of Glenquhorn two years later. Other benefices followed, including the Provostship of St. Giles, Edinburgh, in 1501, the year in which he finished *The Palice of Honour*. He translated Ovid's *Ars Amatoria*

during this period, but it has been lost. In 1512 he began his great translation of Virgil's *Aeneid*, and completed it in eighteen months—one of the
greatest translations ever, with some superb poems as original prologues,
the first of which is probably the best piece of criticism in Scots verse.
Two months after he finished it, his two elder brothers died at Flodden,
and his father retired to a religious house where he died of grief in the next
year, 1514. During this period Gawin was a daily counsellor of the
widowed queen—now twenty-three years old, with a number of dead
children behind her and one live one, the future James the Fifth. The new
Earl of Angus, Gawin's nephew, married the queen in 1514: Gawin was
made Abbot of Aberbrothock in the same year. Shortly after, he came
within an ace of the highest clerical position in Scotland when the queen
nominated him for the archbishopric of St. Andrews: but the canons
elected John Hepburn instead. In 1515 the see of Dunkeld fell vacant, and
Gawin was made bishop. Douglas was soon charged with rigging benefices
and imprisoned by the Lords of Council in various castles including
Edinburgh. This degradation seems to have won him some popular
support, and his oppressors, it is said, even began to fear the intervention
of the queen's formidable brother, Henry VIII of England. Gawin was
released and reinstated. He set to work at his bishopric and affairs of state,
and in May 1517 he was one of three ambassadors to France who negotiated
the Treaty of Rouen, an alliance of Scotland and France against the Auld
Enemy, England. Other intrigues and political deals succeeded, but
eventually the house of Douglas was curbed in its bid for power, and
Gawin, 'desolatt and wofull wycht' as he describes himself to Cardinal
Wolsey in a letter from his inn of exile in London, died of plague in
London in 1522—forty-seven years old.

Gawin Douglas was unquestionably a great man and a great scholar-
poet. No man before or since has had such a vast command of the Scottish
language. He was a man of international stature, of universal mind, and
of what we would call very high IQ. His verse, however, is a bit top-
heavy: with more than enough weight of learning and intellect, it is a
bit thin in rhythm—it lacks the easy movement of Henrysoun, the
powerful drive of Dunbar. I said 'scholar-poet' advisedly for this reason:
he was, for all his great stature, a great versifier rather than a poet: a man
of intellect rather than of genius—the divine fire is wanting. Yet it has
been said, defensibly, that his Aeneid is better then even Virgil himself—
another scholar-poet.

SIR DAVID LYNDSAY was born during the reign of the Fourth James,
probably at the family seat of the Mount, near Cupar, Fife. He studied
at St. Andrews, and travelled on the Continent. In 1513 he was an attendant
of James the Fourth, and a tale is told by Pitscottie of how James was

warned in church by some stranger against going to Flodden, and that Lyndsay had tried to detain the man. He held some sort of tutorial post in relation to the young James the Fifth after that time, and was always on intimate terms with that monarch. He became the court herald, known as the Lyon King of Arms, and held the post until his death. He married a lady of the court, but seems to have had no children. Among his courtly duties was that of providing entertainments, and in this capacity he wrote his great play *Ane Satyre of the Thrie Estaitis* which reveals him as an early and ardent reformer and scourge of the Roman Church. He wrote a mass of poetry of much better quality than has been generally admitted, as well as his one great play in verse, and we present some examples of this poetry here. He was a major poet, the most popular before Burns, but not of the quality of any of the best makars, except perhaps in *Squyer Meldrum*.

Of the remaining minor poets who are still in the makars' tradition, SIR RICHARD MAITLAND of Lethington was both a poet himself and a preserver of the poetry of others—we owe him more as a collector than as a poet. He studied at St. Andrews, travelled abroad, studying chiefly law. He became a Lord of Session, Lord Privy Seal, and held other high appointments. The poems we give here are the work of a genuine minor poet of skill and sincerity, the work of a man of learning and deep sense of responsibility.

ALEXANDER SCOTT was the best writer of songs Scotland produced before Robert Burns. Very little is known of him, but he was clearly a layman, probably a minor courtier, and apparently sympathetic to the Reformation. He seems to have lived at Dalkeith, near Edinburgh. He was a true lyric poet of rare genius—passionate, witty, inspired at his best, a superb craftsman, but no mere 'technician'. The poems we give speak for themselves.

A younger contemporary of Scott, we know little more about ALEXANDER MONTGOMERIE, who is in some ways the bigger if not the better poet of the two: but a different kind of poet, anyway. He seems to have been a professional soldier, to have been born in Germany, and he held the rank of captain. He clearly won the patronage of James the Sixth, himself a poet and even more an astute critic and scholar, who appreciated his gifts. He seems to have held a pension at some time, and to have been deprived of it by scheming enemies: like Dunbar's, many of his poems have the note of complaint. He published his major work *The Cherry and the Slae* in 1595. More than this cannot be said with certainty. He was a good poet of minor talent who aspired rather higher than that: but perhaps his chief place in Scots poetry is as a sonneteer, being one of the earliest of the Italian school. This form never seems to have borne much fruit in Scots, in terms of quality, and by far the best of them is by Mark Alexander Boyd.

Of the two remaining poets, ALEXANDER HUME was a minister who took to religious versifying but left us this one superb summer day poem, *Of the Day Estivall*: and MARK ALEXANDER BOYD was the son of Robert Boyd of Pinkill, Ayrshire. Boyd was a rowdy ne'er-do-well as a young man, knocking about the continent, 'rinning fra banc to banc and wod to wod', but eventually took to study and became one of the best Latin poets of his day. All his Scots verse is lost to us except his one great sonnet given here. He was a man of genius rather than of learning, learned though he was in Greek, Latin, and law, and if this poem is typical of his quality, we have lost work of rare and unique genius. His poem is flawed by the last line, which, as Mr. R. L. C. Lorimer has pointed out, is borrowed from Ronsard—the French influence again: 'que l'homme se deçoit/quand plein d'erreur un aveugle il reçoit/pour sa conduite, un enfant pour son maistre' (Qui voudra voir . . .). The last line, to be consistent, would have had to read:

Led be a wife, and teachit be a bairn.

COMMENTARY

37. THE KINGIS QUAIR
May was the month for love in *Amour Courtois*. The garden is also drawn from the *Rose* convention but note the realistic detail. Cupid was god of the garden of love, usually called Amor in the *Rose* poetry. The heraldic beasts are drawn from another medieval source—the Bestiaries. Fortune in medieval theory was a survival of the Latin pagan deity Fortuna, whose symbol was a wheel as mark of inconstancy. The wheel to the medievals symbolized the vanity of earthly things and their instability. As Fortune, the blind deity, arbitrarily turned her wheel, so one was cast up or down, and those who were up could only fall, those who were down could only rise. In the theory of the nine spheres of influence, she had power over all beneath the moon—that is, all earthly things and creatures were subject to her.

44. THE TESTAMENT OF CRESSEID
His 'fenyeit of the new/Be sum poeit' (stanza 10) is typical Henrysoun humour. The court which tries Cresseid is a court of love—it is *Amour Courtois* she sins against, not marriage; 'scho wes untrew'. Cf. 'The goddis wait all your intent' with Matthew 6.8. The 'fickill quheil' is the wheel of Fortune—see above.

64. THE ABBAY WALK
Here and elsewhere, but not as a rule, I stick strictly to the original, to give an impression of the lack of consistency in these texts—not for its quaintness but because it conveys also some sense of the spirit of the originals, and the sense of 'text' is worth developing.

79. HONOUR WITH AGE
Note the 'see of Lollerdry' in stanza 4. Kennedy was orthodox and conservative. In his *Flyting* with Dunbar (see Collected poems of, Faber text) one of his worst accusations against Dunbar is that he is a Lollard.

81. THE GOLDYN TARGE
The 'stern (star) of day' is the sun; 'Lucyne' is the moon; 'rosere' is the garden of the *Rose*, drawn, like the rest of this poem, from *Le Roman*

de la Rose. But note the realistic detail—a Scottish innovation. The style is 'aureate', a term meaning 'made golden', and drawn from the work of *Les Rhétoriqueurs*, and perhaps also the Latin revival then prevalent. This is Dunbar's tour-de-force in romantic poetry, but it is the realistic detail, the high Renaissance colour-sense, which distinguishes it chiefly. The personifications are typical of the *Rose* convention. Note Dunbar's uncertainty of classical background. He seems to mistake Cleo, the muse of history, for a poetry muse; Apollo for a goddess; Tullius (Cicero) for a poet; and not to know that Pallas is the same person as Minerva, Lucina as Diana. Compare Henrysoun's grasp of classical background in Testament.

90. IN SECREIT PLACE THIS HYNDIR NYCHT
This is a take-off of romantic love of the *Amour Courtois* type.

92. THE TRETIS OF THE TUA MARIIT WEMEN AND THE WEDO
This is the only essay in alliterative verse to come down to us from Dunbar, though alliterative romances lingered longer in popularity in Scotland and the north than in the south. It was the type of verse native to Teutonic languages: rhymed metrical verse is a French influence current among the Norman ruling-class in England, and a by-product of the French alliance in Scotland. Dunbar's poetry in general, and much else of the period, shows a clash and resolution of the two strains. Here he is at his most natural in a measure native to his language, free and exuberant almost to a fault. The Chaucer influence was of course Anglo-Norman, ruling-class in form though middle-class in matter. The opening of the poem is typical romantic machinery: the whole poem is a joke against the *Rose* convention. Note—Johne Blunt was a term of derision, as of an uncouth rustic. 'hie burgh landis' meant the high tenements (landis) of the towns. Lumbart was a form of 'Lombard', that people being famous for their banking and financial propensities. The three balls of the pawn-brokers' sign are drawn from the Lombardy coat of arms. The last four lines are typical of Dunbar's sly wit—'sleekit wut', as we call it in Scots.

107. HIS PANEFULL PURS
There is a sexual innuendo here too—the 'purs' is the scrotum. *Cors* (1.22) is a form of cross, i.e. coin. The *ye* of the last stanza is the King.

109. REMONSTRANCE TO THE KING
Note list of tradesmen and such patronized by James IV, and of the types of hanger-on. Dunbar's remarkable assessment of his own worth is an understatement—his own work has long outlasted most of theirs.

The extraordinary threat to the king at the end is in the old bardic tradition —he is threatening the king with the once-dreaded bardic curse on those who ill-treated the bard.

111. OF A DANCE IN THE QUENIS CHALMER

Sir John Sinclair was a real courtier. Robert Shaw was a physician at court. Stra(th)naver is in Sutherland. Almaser means Almoner. John Bute also was a real courtier. Maestres Musgraeffe was probably the wife of Sir John Musgrave—Dunbar seems to have been in love with her. Dame Dounteboir was a name applied to ladies in waiting. James Dog was the queen's mastiff-like wardrobe-master. Dunbar has two comic-satiric poems on him.

113. THE PETITION OF THE GRAY HORSE, AULD DUNBAR

Note Dunbar's ability to sustain and tease out an image (of himself as an old horse): this is one of the chief and most unmistakable signs of poetic genius. It is also a test of the reality of the image. Youllis yald—it was customary for patrons to present their protégés or retainers with a new coat at Christmas; failure to do so was a sign of dismissal from service; the cast-off dependent was termed a Yule's jade—an old horse no longer fit for service and turned out to grass. Shoemakers (soutaris) chewed the leather to make it soft. Tailors were called 'seme-bytaris'. The Respontio may have been written by the king—it would not have been above his talents—but if he wrote it, he was a good mimic of Dunbar's style. In any case, for once Dunbar's plea was successful, whether through the excellence of his pleading or through the triviality of the plea is conjectural.

116. TO A LADYE

This exquisite lyric needs little comment. It is a distilled drop of dew from the garden of the *Rose*. We could have done with more such. There may be a pun on 'Merche'—Dunbar belonged to the family of the Earls of March: was the lady one of the reigning earl's household?

117. ON HIS HEID-AKE

This little poem strikes a personal and intimate note almost unknown before Dunbar. It is interesting to reflect that a mere aspirin might have given him relief.

117. MEDITATIOUN IN WYNTIR

Does Dunbar mean that nature denies him courage (1st stanza) to *write* plays, or only to enjoy them? If the former, where are the plays of Dunbar? Note the power of Age's speech in stanza seven.

The refrain is from the Office for the Dead in church liturgy. Lydgate also used it in a poem of his. Sir Hew of Eglintoun married a half-sister of Robert II. He died in *c.* 1375. Heryot is unknown. Andrew of Wyntoun was a monk who wrote the Orygynale Cronykil, somewhere between 1395 and 1424. Johne Clerk may be the poet of that name who has a poem or two in the Bannatyne MS. James Afflek (Auchinleck) is unknown. Sir Richard Holland wrote the *Buke of the Howlat c.* 1482. John Barbour was the author of the *Brus*. Schir Mungo Lokert of the Lee and Clerk of Tranent are unknown. Sir Gilbert Hay translated prose and perhaps the *Buik of Alexander*—floreat *c.* 1456. Blind Hary may have been the author of the *Wallas*, an epic in heroic couplets. He is mentioned by John Major in 1521 as author of *a* Wallas. Sandy Traill is unknown. Patrik Johnestoun may have been the poet of that name who has a poem in the Bannatyne MS. Merseir may have been the author of the three poems by one of that name in Bannatyne MS and one in Maitland MS. Of the two Roulls nothing is known, but in the Bannatyne MS there is 'The Cursing of Sir Johine Rowlis/Upoun the steilaris of his fowlis'. Schir Johne the Ros was Dunbar's 'second' in the Flyting with Kennedy. Stobo was a clerk in the reign of James III. Quintyne Schaw has one poem in Maitland MS: he was Kennedy's 'second' in the Flyting.

The sub-title of this poem is too often forgotten—'Quhen he wes sek'. It is the product of a sick depression, not at all typical of Dunbar's fiery energy.

123. TO THE MERCHANTIS OF EDINBURGH

The Stynkand Styll was a passage between the Luckenbooths (a tenement of shops and such) and the kirk of St. Giles. The Mercat Cross is also near St. Giles. Note Dunbar's railery at the way 'singular (individual) proffeit' is encroaching on the common good—a sign of the rise of capitalism.

128. THE FIRST PROLOGUE

Note Douglas's use of 'Scottis' to describe his language. The passage is of critical interest regarding his aims and methods in translating.

129. THE SEVENTH PROLOGUE

The best original poem. Mars and Saturn (25 and 29) are harbingers of evil in astrology. Note the press of alliteration in this poem. In 94 'a bed' means 'abed'. In line 98 'dyd tak kepe' means 'took note of'. In lines 101–4 he means that the opposition of moon and sun is an astrological ill-omen.

'Hebowd' in 105 means owl, as in French *hibou*. The 'crownyt byrd' in 113 is the cock. Palamedes byrdis, in 119, are cranes. Other difficult words of this and other passages are to be found in the fairly exhaustive glossary provided at the back.

135. THE DREME

This is a longish poem in which Lyndsay early announces his main theme of 'Reformation'. He is the heir of Dunbar's satires and, though less of an artist, more consciously in the European movement for reform. Note how, in the *Complaynt of the Comoun Weill* he takes up Dunbar's term 'singular (individual) proffeit'. Lyndsay was the most popular poet before Burns in Scotland, eclipsing Dunbar probably because he was more of a presbyterian type than the essentially catholic Dunbar.

145. ON THE NEW YEIR 1560

This was the year of the Reformation Settlement in Scotland. Maitland, seeing nothing but war coming of the clash between French-catholic and English-protestant influences, seems to say 'A plague o' both your houses!'

146. SATIRE ON THE AGE

This poem of Maitland's is not unworthy of his master, Dunbar.

150. CHRYSTIS KIRK ON THE GRENE

The reference to *Peblis to the Play* in line 4 proves that this is a later poem in the same form modelled on the Peblis one.

165. THE NICHT IS NEIR GONE

An old song re-made by Montgomerie. Dunbar mentions it as a hackneyed popular song in his poem *To the Merchantis of Edinburgh*.

167. THE CHERRY AND THE SLAE

This is a lengthy allegorical poem about aiming high or settling for a compromise lower down the scale. It is his chef-d'oeuvre, and was composed to the tune and stanza of the *Banks of Helicon* which may have been his own invention, or part his and part the music master's of the Royal Chapel. The stanza was given new force by Burns.

173. OF THE DAY ESTIVALL

'Estivall' is simply a Latinism for 'summer'.

176. SONET OF VENUS AND CUPID

The sonnet form seems not to have had much success in Scotland, although many hundreds of them were written. There is room for a study of this matter, as of so much else of Scots literature in the tortured seventeenth century. Who but a Scotsman would think of calling Venus, as Boyd does here, a 'wife'? He is using the word here in its original meaning of woman, although Venus was the faithless wife of Vulcan.

SOME FEATURES OF SCOTS

MIDDLE SCOTS (linguists discern an Early, Middle, and Modern period, roughly corresponding to pre-1424, when James I returned to Scotland; from that date to 1603 and later; and from then to the present) observed the distinction between present participle and gerund by giving the one the ending *-and*, while the other had *-ing* as in English. The gerundial form tended to encroach on the participial *-and*, until the latter was preserved only in speech in certain areas. 'The growand boy loves the fishing.'

Past participles end in *-t*, *-it*, *-d*, or *-ed*: but the first two are commonest. 'He larn*t* that whether rain slopp*it* doun aa day or it snaw*ed* aa nicht, the cairt gae*d* best on wheels.' Euphony is often the best guide here, but usage too.

The verb *gar* implying compulsion or causation, equivalent of causative *make*—'I made him pick it up'—is very common. 'I gart send a man to gar him come and gar her pick it up.' This is common to all periods.

The word *this* takes the plural *thir* (these) and *that* takes the plural *thae* (those) or *thai*, *tha*, etc. Confusion may arise between *thae* for those and the same form for *they*.

Forms for *who* are commonly *quha* or *quhae*, with *wha* or *whae* in modern period: *whose* is *quhase*, *quhais* or the like, with *whase* in modern period. *Which* is *quhilk*, but *that* or *what* or *at* are often used instead.

To, *til*, and *till* are variously used for the English *to*, with *tae* for *too* or *also*. 'Till argue is to fight, and what fighting leads til, tae.'

The commonest plural ending of nouns is *-is*, which is also used for the second person singular of the verb. 'Thou callis the cowis frae the hill.' The *i* is rarely pronounced but occasionally in verse it fills out the metric.

The indefinite article *ane* is a common literary affectation for the early *a*: *ae* or *yae* is an intensive use: *ane* is properly the form for *one* and *one* is often identified with *a*.

Scots verbs take the negative particle *-na*: 'We arena fou, we're no that fou.' The word *no* is the normal negative where English would be *not*, with *nae* where English would be *no*: *nae* has the form *na* commonly also.

Scots loves diminutives which may be multiplied ad absurdum: e.g. *Lass* gives *lassie, lassockie, bit lassockie, wee bit lassockie, wee tottie bit lassockie, wee wee tottie bit*, etc.

Or is commonly used for *before* (*ere* in English).

Than is commonly expressed by *na* or *nor*—'the boy was quicker nor me'.

In pronunciation, the guttural is always sounded—*nicht, loch, nocht*, etc. Medial *v* is rarely sounded—*devil* is *deil*, i.e. medial *l* in the middle period diphthongises—*goldyn* is *gowdin, wolf wowf*. Final *l* may have a similar effect—*knoll* is *knowe, all* is *aw, fall* is *faw*. Liquid *l* and *n* are seen in such words as *tailyeour* and *senyeit* (signed). Metathisis of *r* is common—*gress* (grass) becomes *gerss, thrissil* (thistle) *thirssil*. In general, the English *o* long is *ai* in Scots: *more, mair; floor, fluir (flair); sore, sare*, etc.

GLOSSARY

A

abaising, abashing, lowering
abaisit, abashed
abraid, took leave, abroad
abulyement, habiliment
adew, adieu
afald, singular, concentrated
aigit, aged
air, early
aithis, oaths
alawe, below
alblastrye, missiles
allther, of all
amene, amenable (person)
amyable, sweetheart
anamalit, enamelled
anewis, rings (anneaux)
armypotent, strong in arms
artilye, artillery
assailit, attempted
astert, avoid
aucht, ought, owns
aver, avoir, nag (horse)
avysit, advised, addressed

B

baid, ordered, dwelt, awaited
baill, sorrow
baith, both
balas, Balassian rubies
ballingaris, ships
balme, balm
ban, curse
band, bond
barkit, clotted

barlaw fummill, call for truce
barrat, trouble
barrow trammis, barrow shafts
baty bummill, bungler
bawch, useless
bawchles, documents
bawsy, ballsy
be, being
begaryit, smeared, mottled
begouth, begowthe, begin
behuffit, behoved
beild, shelter
beir, rasping noise, to sing, barley, bear
beirit, bellowed
beit, supply
bek, tusk, beak
bellie blind, blind man's buff, completely blind
bellyhuddrun, glutton
belyve, quickly
beriall, beryl
bernis, men
beswik, cheat
beugh, bough
bewis, boughs
bewrie, reveal, confess
bickerit, fought, struck
bigging, building
bikkir, assault
birnying, burning
birs, bristles
blaiknit bair, desolate
blawis, blows
blenking, expression

blent, glanced
blerde, bleared
blomyt, bloomed
blonkis, white horses
blynis, cease
bo, make a face
boddum, valley floor
bogill, spectre
bone, bare
boudyn, swollen
bougaris, rafters
boun, ready
bourd, joke
bosteous, boustious, busteous,
   boisterous
bowk, body
bowis, bows, sticks
bownyt, made ready
bowster, bolster
braid, broad
brane wode brynt in bales,
   firewood burnt in bundles
brankand, swaggering
brast, burst
(on) breid, abroad
(on) breird, aburgeon
bremys, breams
brent, smooth
brichtest, most beautiful
briggis, bridges
broud, dote, embroider
browdin, smeared
browderit, doted
bruike, bruke, brook
brukkill, brukle, fragile, frail
brumaill, wintry
bryght, bricht, beauty
brylyoun, ?
brym, fierce
bubbis, squalls, blasts
buddis, bribes
bumbart, drone

bukky, tongue in cheek
bullar, bubble
burd, board
bure, bore
burelie, stoutly
buskit, dressed
bushment, ambush
but, without
bute, buit, remedy
buthman, boothman
buttrie, bucket

C

cabeld, haltered
caf, chaff
cair weid, mourning clothes
(on) caiss, perchance
cald, cold, rheum
cale, cabbage-soup
callour, fresh
camscho, crooked
camow-nosed, hook-nosed
capirculyoun, capercailzie
cappill, horse
carling, old woman
carll, old man
carpit, chatted
carybald, cannibal
cassin, cast
causay, causeway
cavell, fellow
cawandaris, ?
celicall, heavenly
chaftis, cheeks
chaip, escape
chamelot, camlet cloth
(on) char, ajar
charde, pierced
chat, hang
cheir, pierce
chesit, chose
cheverit, shook

chuf, churl
chymmys, buildings
chyvirrand, shivering
claggit, clogged
clatteraris, tattlers
clayis, clothes
cleik, claw
cleir, beautiful
cleuch, cliff
claver, clever, clover
clevering, clinging
clymbare, climber
clype, softie
coist, coast
colleveris, coal-heavers
comptit, counted
conding, excellent
consuetude, custom
contrair, against
conyng, learned, rabbit
cop, cowp cup
cought, could
counterfutit France, imitated
    Fr. dance
courtyns, curtains
cout, colt
covece, covetousness
cowhubye, booby
craikiris, boasters
craudoune, coward
croppis, shoots
crose, croce, cross, coin
crowdie mowdie,? mouldy cheese
crudis, curds
cruik, hook
crynd, withered
cubok, cabok, cheese
cummar, to encumber
cummerans, encumbrance
cummerlik, neighbourly
cunyng, rabbit
cunyouris, coiners

curage, stamina
curall, coral
curches, kerchiefs
cure, care
curldodie, species of plant
cursouris, coursers
curtly, courtly
cussat, wood-pigeon

D

daill, deal
daine, dane, haughty
dalis, deals, lots
damys, pisses
dang, struck, overcome
darflie, boldly
darth, death
dasyng, dazing
dauphin, dolphin
daynte, esteem
degoutit, spotted
deid, deed, death
deir, daunt
denger, danger
depurit, purified
deray, commotion, revelry
dern, secret
dery dan(toun), copulation,
    sexy dance
deval, to descend
diches, ditches
dicht, dressed
digne, worthy
dill, relieve
dink, denk, fine, prim
dirkin, darken(ing)
discryve, describe
disjone, to breakfast; separate
dispone, prepare
dissaive, deceive
dissimulence, dissimilation
dissymyland, dissembling

dogonis, nobodies
doif, dowf, sad
dollin, delved, buried
donk, wetted, dank
doolie, doleful
dosk, dusk(y)
dotit, doted, fond, stupid
dour, hard, unyielding
dowis, doves
dree, drie, endure
(bot) dreid, without fear
drublie, wet
druggar, drudging
druggit, dragged
drumly, to muddy
drup(e), droop, feeble
dubbis, puddles
dule, sorrow
duleful, doleful
dungin, overcome, put down
duntis, jolts
dures, injury
duris, doors
dyk, ditch, wall
dyte, poem
dyting, writing
dyvour, bankrupt

E

edderis, adders
effeiris, bearing, affairs
eft, afterwards
eftsones, soon after
eirdly, earthly
eirrand, errand, arrant, erring
eldnyng, jealousy
elrich, supernatural, wild
emerant, emerald
enbroudin, embroidered
enchessoun, cause, dissent
endlang, along
endyte, to write, writing

engyn, engine, genius
enlumynit, illumined
ennoyt, annoyed
erd, earth
etlit, attempted
exeme, examine
expone, expound
evour, ivory

F

(but) fabill, frankly
fa(l)cheoun, cutlass
fader, father
failyait, failed
fane, fain, weather-vane
fangis, seizes, holds
farcy, diseased
farnys, ferns
fawch, dirty yellow
fay, forth
fe, sheep, hire
feill, feel, smell, many
feir, fear, companion
feirris, appearance
felloun, deadly
felterit, tangled
fepillis, pouts
ferlifull, wonderful
fervent, hot
fessoun, fashion
fetrit, fettered
feynit, feigned
flaggis, flashes
flanis, flans, arrows
flasche, quiver
flauchter falis, long turfs
flaw, squall
fleichouris, sycophants
flemit, put to flight
flete, flow, float
flingaris, dancers

194

floschis, swamps
flume, river
flyrit, grimaced
flyte, to rail, debate
fone, foes, to fool
forfochin, exhausted
forky, stalwart
forlane, forlorn
forleit, forsake, forget
forloir, forsake(n)
(a) forrow, before
forsy, strong
forquhy, because
foulis, fowls
foutht, abundance
fow, full
foynyee, beech marten
frak, active
frawart, perverse
fray, fright
freke, manly man
fremyt, foreign, strange
fret, freit, gnaw, interlace, omen
frigs, fellows
fruster, impotent
frutles, barren
fu(i)lyeit, worn out
fumyll, fumble
fure, fellow
futher, myriad

G

gadderit, gathered
gadman, teamster
gair, gusset
gaipis, strive(s)
gaitis, goats
gammaldis, gambols
gammis, gums
gane, face
ganecome, return
ganest, most fitting

ganyies, darts
ganyt, suited
gar, make, compel
gart, gert, compelled
garth, garden
gavell, rascal
gawfe, guffaw
gayte, goat
geir, goods
geit, jet
generabill, created
gent, beautiful
gentryce, noble birth
gers, gris, grass
gesserant, shining mail
geummill, interfere
gib, tom-cat
gif, if, given
giglotlike, whorelike
gillot, mare
girn, complain
gird, to rail
gladderrit, besmeared
glading, cheering
glaid, glad
glaikis, boasters, folly
glar, glaur, mud
gled, kite
gledaris, obscure
glete, glitter
glewis, sports
gleyd, ember
glowrand, glaring
gobbis, mouths
goif, gove, stare
goulis, red
gousty, dismal
grane, colour, groan
granis, groans
grathit, graithit, dressed
gravin, buried
greis, degrees

greking, dawn
grete, great, weep
grew, Greek
grome, man
grouf, prostrate
groukaris, ?
gryce, sow
guckit, foolish
gurl, stormy
gutaris, gutters
gyane, giant
gyis, gyse, manner, play
gymp, neat

H

habirgeoun, mail-coat
hable, fit
hace, hoarse
hache, ache, pain
haik, lazy beast
hailland, hauling
hair, hoary
hait, hot, jot, hate
halk, hawk
hals, throat
haly, holy, wholly
hanyt, saved
harsk, harsh
hasart, grey
haw, livid
hautand, haughty
Hebowd, a proper name
hechar, higher
hecht, named, promised
heich, high
heildit, covered
heis, upraises
heithing, mockery
heklis, rubs with heckle
heklit, hackled
helit, covered, healed
hely, highly

hensour, scapegrace
herknere, listening
herle, heron
heryit, harried
hete, heat, hate
hewmond, helmet
heylis, neck
heynd, hende, gentle, skilled
hidlis, hiding places
hie, he, high
hippit, hopped
hirpilland, limping
hissill, hazel
hoddous, hideous
hogeart, ? huckster
hoir, rough
holsum, badger
holttis, woods
hommiltye jommeltye,
   ? shambling
(but) hone, at once
hortis, hurts
hostit, coughed
howffing, booby
howis, legs
howt, a wood
hufing, lodging
huiche, cliff
hur, whore
hurcheone, hedgehog
hurle, diarrhoea
hutit, hooted, ? hated
huttock, a fancy cap
hy, haste
hyndir, yester
hyne, hence, afar
hynt, took
hyrnys, hiding places

I

iatouris, tale-tellers
impesh, hinder

inthrang, pressed in
ische, issue
ische schouchlis, icicles

J

jangill, gossip
janglour, tattler
josit, enjoyed
juffler, shuffler
jymp, taunt

K

kay, jackdaw
keip, care
kell, woman's cap
kemmit, combed
kene, sharp, alert
kerffis, carves
kest, cast
keyth, kyth, reveal
kie, kye, cattle, ? kid
kirsp, fabric
kirtillis, skirts
kith, race
kitties, small Kates, girls
knaip, boy, servant
knapping, budding
knopis, buds
knyp, nibble
kokenis, ? coquins

L

laggerit, bemired
laif, lave, remainder, rest
lair, lore
laist, held
laittis, habits
lampis, gallops
lance, fiddle
landwart, rural
larbaris, impotent men
lat, prevent

lathit, loathed
laton, brass
lattit, prevented
law, law, low
lawte, lawtie, fidelity
leid, leyd, folk, tongue, lead, lover
leill, loyal
lemand, glowing
lemman, lover
lemys, glows
lendis, loins
lestis, lasts
lesty, skilful
lettis, pretends
lettron, lectern
levefell company, lawful company
levin, lightning
leys, pastures
lichtlyit, despised
lig, (to) lie
liggit, lain
lincum, lincoln
ling, heather-patch
list, listis, desire(s)
lob, clumsy
loppin, leapt
losingeris, deceivers
loun, lowne, creature, lad
lourand, skulking
lous, louse, loose(n)
lousit, unloosed
lufare, lover
lufe, luve, love
luggit, pulled by ears
luknyt, locked
lumbart, banker, (Lombard)
lume, tool, penis
lustis, desires
lusty, pleasant, a beauty
lyart, hoary

lykand, liking
lynd, lime-tree, linden
lynnys, weirs
lyre, skin
lyte, little
lyth, listen

M

maculait, spotted, soiled
maggit, heaped
magrayme, migraine
maik, mate
maikless, matchless
maistrye, sovereignty
makaris, poets
makis, mates, composes
malis, burden
manace, menace
maner, manner
mangit, loaded, mangy
mantill, mantle
mapamoud, world
mart, beef
martrik, marten
matutyne, (of) morning
matyne, morning
mawgre, despite, ill-will
mawis, mavis, thrush
medis, meadows
meid, reward
meirswyne, porpoise
mekle, mekill, much
mellit, mingled
menskit, honoured
menyie, company
merle, blackbird
merrens, ? murrain
merse, mast-button
midis, myddis, middle, midst
mingit, mingled
mo, more
mokis, mocks

molet, bridle-bit
mon, must
mortfundit, benumbed
mot, may
mottie, spotted
mowaris, jokers
mowis, joke(s)
mowlit, mouldy
moy, tame, mild
moyne, moon
mudlit, threw
munyoun, minion
murgeound, derided
murthir, murder
mychane, ? mouth
myddyng, midden
mynnye, mother
mystirs, wants, needs

N

na, than
nar, near
neiff, neive, fist
neip, turnip
nevell, punch
(them) nicht, nigh them
nobbit, knocked
noddill, pate
nowis, heads
noy, annoyance
nureis, nurse, nourish

O

oblissing, obligation
offusked, darkened
oiss, use
oist, host
Omer, Homer
onrycht, awry
or, before, than
oratur, oratory
orlager, clock, timepiece

our, over, too
ourgilt, gilded over
ourhailing, turning over
ourheild, cover(ed) over
outwaill, outcast
owk, week
oxster, armpit

P

paikis, deserts
pako, peacock
pansch, tripe
pansing, thinking
panton, slipper
papinjay, parrot
pappis, breasts
partand, parting
patill, plough-staff
pedder, peddlar
peir, peer, equal
pend, close, archway
pene, penis
peronall, young girl
persave, perceive
pertlyar, livelier
pillie, ?
plank, ? small coin
platfut, flat-footed
pleid, dispute
plet, plaited
pley, plea
pleyne, play, complain
plich (ankers), sheet anchor
possodie, sheeps-head broth
preif, preve, prove
preiss, share
pres, crowd
prettick, fine
propone, propose
prunya, preen
pulder, powder
pungitive, threatening

purpur, purple
put, thrust
pykis, spikes

Q

quhair, book
quhalis, whale's
quhele, wheel
quhilk, which
quhill, while, until
quhillelillie, penis
quhyt, white

R

rad, afraid
raffel, doeskin
ragment, catalogue
raik, graze
raith, early
rakit, raked
rakles, reckless
ralyeit, railed, joked
rankild, rankled
rap, beat
raucht, reached
ravin, raven(ing)
raw, together
reboytit, repulsed
rebute, rebuttal
red, tidy up
rede, completely
redis, reeds
rege, quarrel
reird, noise
reke, smoke
rele, go round
remufe, remove
renk, deed, person
repatyrit, fed
responsaill, responsible, sub-
  stantial
reulit, ruled

reullie, tractable
revin, rewin, riven
revis, robs
rew, pity
riall, royal
riggis, spines
rinkis folk, deeds
rise, brushwood
rispis, sedges, straw
roch, rough
rockis, distaffs
roi, king
rone, rowan
ronk, rank
ronys, thickets
rosere, rose-garden
roust, ? disturbance, rust
rousty, hoarse, rusty, quarrelsome
rownis, whispers
rowtting, rutting
ruch, rough
rude, cheek
rufill, ruffle
rummill, range
rungis, cudgels
rusing, boasting
ryce, grove
ryng, reign

S

saifit, saved
sain, sane, bless, make sign of
    Cross
saits, seats
sakles, innocent
salbe, shall be
salt, assault
saluse, salute
sanyne, blessing
sanitive, healthful
sapher, sapphire
sark, shirt

sary, feeble, sorry
sat, set, suited
sathanas, Satan's
saw, sow, saying
scaffaris, beggars
(our) scalit, scaled over, spilled
    over
scaith, harm
scamleris, spongers
scantlie, scarcely
scart, scratch
schaiffyne, shaven
schalk, churl
schaw, covert, reveal
schein, schene, beautiful
schent, destroyed
schevill, wry
schomd, ? shorn, ? combed
schowis, shoves
schrenk, shrink
schrowd, dress
schupe, set about
schyre, sheer
scippis, ships
scrippit, jeered
scunner, revulsion
scutarde, beshitten
sege, say, man
seilis, seals (legal)
seip, seep
seir, several
sely, blessed
semely, lady
semit, seemed
sen, since
sene, seyne, to say
setten, make fast
settis, suits
sextie, sixty
sic, sike, such, sigh, sick, stream
(of) sicht, at sight
sickir, certain

200

sile, hide
skabbit, scabby
skailis, flecks, spills
skant, wanting, scarce
skarth, cormorant
skeich, shy
sker, scare(d)
skrip, scrip
skug, shade
slawsygawsy, ? sluggard
sle, subtle
sloknyt, slaked
sloppare, slippery
smaikis, mean fellows
smake smolet, ? wretched leer
smaragdyne, emerald
smy, wretch
snell, keen, bitter
snypand, biting
solsequium, sunflower
sone, soon, sun
soukaris, suckers
soutter, shoemaker
sowklar, sucker
sowpit, drenched
soyr, sorrel
spald, joint
spanit, weaned
splene, heart
spraings, shoots
spreit, spirit
spruning, sprung
spuilyeit, spoiled
spynist, blown open
stacker, stagger
standar, standing
stune, penis
stanneris, pebbles
stendis, strides
stent, stopped
stern, star
stew, ? bung

stingis, spikes
stirk, bullock
stoppil, stopper
storkyn, stiffen
stottis, bullocks
stoure, strife
straik, stroke
straitis, leather, felt
streiking, stretching
strekyt, stretched
strumill, ? gelded
stryp, rill
stunyst, stunned, astonished
styll, market
stythly, stiff(ly)
sudroun, English
sugeorne, delay
sulyie, soil
swak, thud
swalme, swelling
swanking, ? gallant
swanquhit, swanwhite
swapit, swished
swelt, fainted
swentyouris, swyngeouris,
    rogues
swerf, faint
sueving, dream(ing)
swonne, swoon
swyr, ? hill-pass
swyth, quick, at once
sye, saw
sylit, hidden
syng, sign
syse, time(s)
syte, sorrow

T

taburne, tabor
taftais, taffeta
takyn, token
temit, emptied

tendit, tended
tene, anger, rage
tent, care, heed
teris, tears
terne, trouble, fierce
thai, thae, those
thains, ?
thak, thatch
thir, their, these
thoillit, endured
thonk, thanks
thoume, thumb
thra, boldly
thrall, serf
thrawe, space, while
thrimlaris, tremblers
thristaris, thrusters
tolter, tatter
towdie, ? female genitalia
to wrye, utterly twisted
traist, trust
trane, snare
trawe, trick
trist, tryst
trone, weighing-machine
tryackill, potion
*tuchan, stuffed calf-skin
tume, empty
turse, dress
turtouris, turtle-doves
tyk(e), cur, mongrel
tyndis, antler-tines
tyrliemyrlie, ?
to tyne, to lose
tynt, lost
tyt, presently, soon

U

ugsum, ugly
unfane, displeased
unfulyeit, unsoiled

ungird, unguarded
unyoldin, unyielded

V

vanegloir, vainglory
vardour, verdure
varie, shake
ventositeis, gusts of wind
vitre, glass
vively, vividly
voce, voice
voidis, voids

W

wait, know(s)
waill, wale, choose
walknit, wakened
wallidrag, weakling
walliegowdie, jewel
wally, wavy
walteris, welters
walx, wax, grew
wambe, belly
wan- prefix 'un', wanthrift, e.g.
wanhope, despair
wanis, house(s)
wariand, cursing
waris, curses
warlie, warly, warily, warlike
warpit, uttered, wrapped
wattir broks, ? otters
wauchtit, drank
wed, weed
wedder, sheep, weather
(lusty in to) wedis, gaily dressed
wedow, widow
weid, dress
weir, war, (to) defend
wekit, wicked
wellis, ?wells, ? hollows
welterit, floundered, upset

* Used to make cows give milk.

wend, thought
werely, warlike
wery eftir couth weip, weary
   and like to weep
weyis, weighs, ways
wicht, wight, stalwart man
wicker, willow
wilyco(i)t, waistcoat
wit, know
wlonkes, beauties
wobat, caterpillar
wod, wid, mad, wood
wolroun, glutton
wonne, dwell, won
worthit, became
wortis, plants
wosp, bung
wote, knows
wowit, wooed
wraikfull, vengeful

wrinkis, tricks
wrokin, avenged
wyppit, tied
wysnyt, wizened
wyt, wyte, wite, blame

Y

yaip, eager
yald, jade
yeid, went
yeild, impotent
yemit, intended
yerd, penis
yerne, desire
yet(tis), gate(s)
yfere, companionable
yoldin, yielded
yowtheid, youth
ysoupit, drenched
ythrungin, thrust up

INDEX OF TITLES AND FIRST LINES
OF POEMS

0